ESSAYS

from Zimbabwe

ESSAYS
from Zimbabwe

By Parker T. Williamson

Executive Editor
The Presbyterian Layman

Contents

From Harare, Zimbabwe, site of the 50th anniversary Jubilee Assembly of the World Council of Churches, Parker T. Williamson filed an essay severely critical of Zimbabwe President Robert Mugabe. A copy of the report was sent to Lloyd Lunceford, chairman of the Publications Committee of the Presbyterian Lay Committee and a specialist in communications law. Lunceford was worried – not because of the content of the column but because of the character of Mugabe.

In Zimbabwe, people who oppose Mugabe often wind up dead.

Lunceford feared that Zimbabwe officials might monitor The Layman Online, the official web site of the Presbyterian Lay Committee, where Williamson's accounts were posted on a daily basis during his coverage of the World Council of Churches. Therefore, the attorney advised the Lay Committee to hold Williamson's essay on Mugabe until after he was safely aboard a return flight to the United States.

Williamson responded quickly to that advice, asserting that he was in Zimbabwe to cover the news and that what he saw and read needed to be told. Lunceford and the Lay Committee staff relented. *Reflections on Zimbabwe,* Williamson's first report from Zimbabwe, was posted on the web site, and readership statistics began to soar. That essay, and others written during his coverage of the World Council of Churches Assembly December 3-14, 1998, comprise the content of this book. Williamson did, in fact, return home safely, but also sheepishly. Yes, there were real dangers for a journalist writing disparagingly of the government of Robert Mugabe. "When Patty and I passed through the government's final gauntlet at the Harare Airport and boarded British Airways, I breathed a prayer of thanks," Williamson said. *[Shortly after Williamson returned to the United States, two Zimbabwean journalists were arrested by the Zimbabwe government and tortured. See Postscript, page 79.]*

The World Council of Churches played it safe, taking no action that risked Mugabe's disapproval or retaliation. Konrad Raiser, general secretary, explained to the press that it was a policy of the WCC not to criticize host governments. But the WCC not only failed to criticize Mugabe, it also endorsed his socialist economics and land redistribution schemes. It accepted his view that global economies and transnational corporations were destroying his nation's economy without examining Mugabe's policies that have driven his people further into poverty. The council took the road it has taken so often in the past quarter-century, advocating socialism, liberation theology and an aberrant version of the Christian faith, from which the WCC sprang.

Both as a Presbyterian minister and a journalist, Williamson has been a long-time critic of the World Council of Churches – but not from the beginning. He reminds readers that the council began in Europe out of the ashes of World War II as a noble effort to bring the reconciliation of Jesus Christ and the hope of the Gospel to a war-torn world. He shows that unity among Christians – the founding vision of the WCC – grew out of a passion for missions. In contrast to that dream, Williamson's accounts demonstrate how today's World Council of Churches has lost sight of its ideal and continues careening away from the claims of the gospel.

Essays from Zimbabwe is a rich mixture of reports – straight news, analyses, essays and wry humor. They provide much more than an account of events and decisions that sprang from the Jubilee Assembly. They go behind the scenes and explain how and why the World Council of Churches continues to stray from its original mission.

Presbyterians need to understand the World Council of Churches. The Presbyterian Church (USA) contributes more financial support to the World Council of Churches than any other U.S. denomination. The denomination's stated clerk, the Rev. Clifton Kirkpatrick, is a member of the WCC's Central Committee, which governs the organization until its next assembly seven years from now. Presbyterians need to reassess the level of this support for the WCC and the manner in which their delegates acceded to the WCC's misguided policies.

We pray that this book will help inspire a zeal for proclaiming the Christian faith, whether from within the WCC or apart from it.

> "O Lord. To what a state dost
> Thou bring those who love thee."
> *St. Teresa of Avila, The Interior Castle*

To reflect coherently upon so large an event as that of the late Assembly of the World Council of Churches in Harare can never be easy as, of necessity, there are so many competing images, not to mention the forests of documents and plethora of statements to which one might refer. Naturally, certain moments stand out, such as that of the standing ovations for Comrade President Mugabe, the Africanized liturgies with keyboards and the dramatic gesture of those who sought to advance the cause of indigenous peoples everywhere with enhanced integrity by taking all their clothes off. Yet to speak thus is to risk trivializing just what all this commotion, and the gathering of around 5,000 people from more than 339 denominations was supposed to be about: nothing less than the visible Unity of the entire Christian Church.

Earthly concerns

The manifest unrealizability of this goal at present is perhaps among the factors that allows the World Council to devote itself to so many other things along the way. Thus it is in the interim, before the parousia of global Christian unity is attained, that the WCC has taken up with particular zeal such concerns as have come to prominence in purely secular circles: the role of women (as understood in a particular feminist sense), minorities, the "differently-abled" and certain indigenous peoples. In addition, there is a pervasive but unquestioned commitment to the criticism of economic development, capitalism, "globalization" (whatever that is), and the use (always referred to as "exploitation") of the earth's mineral and other resources.

Singing in the rain

An ultimate Malthusian pessimism thus travels in yoke to a simultaneous and ultimately secular optimism about the inevitable triumph of liberal goals and values. Since there are incommensurable differences between the worldviews of the participants, the WCC can thus only be an umbrella under which some participants are going to get wet. The language of crisis is highly appropriate in its theological sense: where concepts are in tension because their unity cannot be thought. I now turn my attention to the single most effective group in the World Council, by which I mean, of course, the leadership and administration. One cannot help but admire the efficiency of this group. Apart from occasional disruptions and contumacy, the ideological grip of the Geneva-based bureaucrats was pervasive, if not entirely absolute.

Divide and conquer

Indeed it is a tribute to their genius that they devised the program known as the *padare* [fragmenting the assembly into single-interest discussion groups], as this gave all of the hundreds of lobbyists and pressure groups their moment in the sun. The *padare* ran for several days but was in fact quite unconnected to the rest of the assembly. Nonetheless most of the groups involved went away happy, in the curious belief they had been heard and made their point, when in fact most of them had achieved nothing at all.

It is plain that unity in terms of common assent to doctrinal truths is not a model that the leadership in general and General Secretary Konrad Raiser in particular found acceptable. Indeed Dr. Raiser seemed quite comfortable with the suggestion that for the WCC, when it comes to unity, it is better always to travel than to arrive. "I would be pretty suspicious of any understandings that visible unity is a state of affairs that is once arrived at and then you maintain it. ... I would prefer to consider church unity much rather as a process, and therefore in the image of the journey of the pilgrimage ... than as the static institutional understanding of unity."

Negotiating truth

The traditional Anglicans, the Orthodox and the evangelicals have made it clear that they all feel marginalized in the WCC. When it was suggested that perhaps the common factor among these groups was that they felt there were some truths that were not negotiable, Dr. Raiser responded that such an attitude was indeed a problem. As he observed, "if you defend a line of exclusive truth beyond which no dialogue is possible, I mean you either accept that basis, or you have to leave it, and that makes it difficult to stay with the painful and laborious process of ecumenical and counter-exchange dialogue."

Raiser's reply lays bare the ideological problem at the heart of the whole WCC project, as the organizers conceive it. It suggests that there should be a warning over the entrance to the headquarters in Geneva: "Abandon doctrine all ye who enter here." After all, in the promised land of the WCC, the only dogmas will be social, political and ethical, while there is more than a suggestion that it is only really through these avenues that the Kingdom of God on earth will ever arrive anyway. In every sense this is a theology of ideology where all is understood as ultimately mundane.

Making space for Jesus

If all this seems to amount to a rather extreme interpretation, it needs to be acknowledged that there was also in use at the WCC the more familiar language regarding Jesus Christ. But the feeling was conveyed that this use is concessive and should not be seen as strictly necessary, since it is uncomfortably exclusive: those who wish may speak of Jesus, but they should not require it of others.

In demonstration of this reasoning there remains one final conceptual shift to notice. This begins with the view, quietly laid out in recent key WCC documents, that it may be inappropriately limiting to see the WCC as merely Christian. Thus Dr. Raiser pointed out in his address to the assembly, that to state as the document "Towards a Common Understanding and Vision of the WCC" does, that ecumenical space is a space where "the Churches can explore (together) what it means to be in fellowship towards greater unity in Christ" (CUV para. 3.5.4) "does not transcend the perspective of inter-church ecumenism." Therefore, Dr. Raiser has proposed that "the ecumenical space will have to be opened for the concerns of the world."

Lest this be thought too vague, Dr. Raiser makes his aim clearer by quoting Peter Lodberg's view that "The WCC is a sanctuary in a divided world" and he then explains this by saying that "A sanctuary is a place of refuge for the stranger, it offers hospitality to those who have no home." Finally, he quotes with approval a passage from the revealingly titled book by L. Mudge, *The Church as a Moral Community* (Geneva, 1982, p. 112). There, Mudge declares that "Churches can and should offer a sort of metaphorical space in the world for those, believers or otherwise, who believe that human society can overcome its violent origins, its continuing resentment and mistrust ... "

Transcending Christianity

Although it seemed to pass with little comment, it is surely hard to overstate the significance of this position by WCC leaders, for it lays the groundwork for the WCC to let go of mere Christianity for the embrace of the world. All of which takes us back to the "anthropological critique" of Feuerbach. Here is conceived a cosmos where it is not so much man made in the image of God as God in the image of man as realized in community. It is little wonder that Dr. Raiser finds denominations constricting when it is Christianity itself he would have us transcend. Amidst such thinking it was refreshingly candid of the moderator, His Holiness Aram I, The Catholicos of Cilicia, to join the list of those who see a crisis in the WCC. In his report to the assembly he suggested that the crisis will not be remedied by backsliding into the morass of mere theology or the darkness of primitive faith. Instead, the future lies with the structural, the political, the social and the economic: "In its formative years the Council was mainly preoccupied with the theological and doctrinal issues." But now "issues related to unity and questions pertaining to society can no longer be treated separately, they must be seen in their dynamic and inseparable inter-connectedness. We have achieved this insight in the last decade and should continue to build on it." He encouraged the churches to remember that "the forces of racism, social, economic and political marginalization and the destructive repercussions of globalization need to be countered with the churches' resolute witness to the liberating news of God's inclusive and reconciling love for all people and the whole of creation."

The irony is that all this evolving ideology generates its own problems for the WCC administration: how to liberate itself from the remaining formal bonds imposed by its theoretical subservience to the member churches. Happily for the leadership, it has found a strategy – eloquently captured in the rhetoric of the General Secretary himself: "Enlarge the space for your dwelling. Extend the curtains of your tent ..." (Isaiah 54.2).

Conflicting visions

There is thus at root in the WCC a clash of two potential hegemonies. One is secular and liberal, seeing the goal of ecumenism as the inclusion of all and the ultimate accommodation of Christianity to the requirements of the non-Christian and the secular. The other is ecclesial, seeing ecumenism as an inter-church dialogue seeking to heal the wounds in the body of Christ so that the way of salvation in Christ should be the better available to all. Clearly the first model is in the ascendant among WCC leaders. But the second model surely informs the approaches to ecumenism of many of the historic churches within the WCC. Indeed it is no accident that it is many of those who feel most marginalized from the WCC who share this outlook: the Orthodox, the Anglicans and (from outside) the Roman Catholics and even many of the evangelicals.

The words of the Orthodox Fr. Leonid Kishkovsky are compelling: "We have always lived in the expectation and hope that there is an openness" such that, "those who find a theology, faith – and many fundamental assertions about those things – to be non-negotiable" can "be in one community of dialogue at least and debate with those who feel that everything is negotiable. But if the core principle is that everything is negotiable, then certainly the next decades will show continuing withdrawal on the part of a number of churches."

Another Orthodox church representative, Dr. Paul Meyendorff, has argued that "the liberal Protestant agenda no longer holds sway in the worldwide communion of Churches" and consequently that in the next few years we will see a realignment. If Meyendorff's observations are accurate – and there are strong indicators among the WCC's member churches that they are – it will not be Christianity, but rather the World Council of Churches itself that we shall have learned to transcend.

–Alistair J. Macdonald-Radcliff
Church of England News
London, England

The writer is researching a book on the Christian concept of revelation.

The World Council of Churches, gathering in Harare, Zimbabwe, for its 50th anniversary meeting December 3-14, 1998, has been in this country before. Vicariously, so have I. When the World Council came to Zimbabwe (then known as Rhodesia) in 1978 it brought bullets and bombs. Then, as an elected leader of the Presbyterian Church (US), I could not ignore that act, nor could I turn my back on the fact that contributions from my denomination made it possible. Zimbabwe was a turning point for us all.

In 1978, this African country was engaged in turbulent transition. Colonialist Ian Smith's regime had finally come to terms with the fact that white people alone could no longer rule this fabulously wealthy land. Gold emerged from the ground. Farms exported their bounty throughout Africa. Game parks attracted tourists worldwide. Transportation, health care, electrification and communication systems were the jewel of the continent. But in spite of all these accomplishments, Rhodesia could not survive while its black population remained disenfranchised. White rule had to end.

But by any rational judgment, Rhodesian blacks, who had long been suppressed, were in no position to run suddenly and without preparation this sophisticated and highly efficient infrastructure. Theirs had been a tribal life, governed by a worldview that could not easily accommodate ideological assumptions on which the Rhodesian economy was formed. So a biracial government was organized, an instrument of transition, an attempt to transfer incrementally the levers of control, to apprentice into leadership a very different people.

The WCC funds revolution

Not so, said the World Council of Churches. The council declared its support for the Patriotic Front, a cluster of guerrilla fighters led by Robert Mugabe and Joshua Nkomo, that had been funded and trained by the Soviet Union, North Korea and Cuba. Mugabe/Nkomo guerrillas demanded an immediate takeover of the biracial Rhodesian regime, and World Council leaders conferred moral legitimacy to their claim.

Tactics of the Patriotic Front were well known by 1978, for in February 1997, according to reports by *Newsweek*, the Patriotic Front had murdered seven Roman Catholic missionaries who opposed its Marxist campaign. Again, in June of 1977, the Patriotic Front killed three men, five women and four children at a Pentecostal missionary post for similar reasons. Reports of these killings notwithstanding, the WCC, in

August 1978, gave the Patriotic Front $85,000 from its Fund to Combat Racism, an account to which the Presbyterian Church had contributed generously. No strings had been attached to the grant. In fact, WCC guidelines specifically prohibited the imposition of such strings, stating in its Notting Hill principles that the grants were to be "made without control over the manner in which they are spent."

The politics of murder

In August, 1978, the same month in which the WCC awarded the grant, the Patriotic Front shot down a civilian Air Rhodesia plane, killing thirty-eight of its fifty-six passengers. *TIME* and *Newsweek* reported in their September 1978 issues that a small group of survivors climbed out of the wreckage and pleaded for mercy, but they were assassinated by Patriotic Front guerrillas using Soviet-made Kalashnikov rifles. According to the accounts, the next day, when Rhodesian troops parachuted into the area, they found ten bodies, including seven women and two young girls, among those who had been gunned down.

Later, when the Patriotic Front won its revolution, largely due to the support it received from Soviet bloc countries and organizations like the World Council of Churches, Zimbabwe's new prime minister, Robert Mugabe, publicly thanked the WCC for its "commitment to the principles for which you and we have struggled together" (Ecumenical Press Service, March 7, 1980). WCC leaders also claimed the victory, with General Secretary Philip Potter vowing triumphantly during the WCC's 1980 General Council meeting that the WCC would "not be bullied by those who attack us for giving our attention to controversial political issues" (Document No. 23, WCC Central Committee, Geneva, 1980, p. 10).

Tribal warfare

Shortly after Mugabe ascended the throne of what was to become his one-party state, he moved to consolidate his power. In January 1982, he turned against his ally, Joshua Nkomo, imprisoned and later exiled him. Then in 1983, in a monumental campaign of genocide, Mugabe unleashed his North Korean-trained Shona tribal warriors on Nkomo's numerically-smaller Matebele tribe, resulting in mass killings throughout Matebeleland.

In that same period, Mugabe ordered a crackdown on the free press throughout Zimbabwe, a control that has never been fully lifted, and a reality of no small concern to some members of the press who entered this country to report on the WCC meeting.

Thus two former allies would experience reunion as the World Council visited Zimbabwe. Both Mugabe and the WCC have undergone radical changes since their revolutionary partnership was consummated in 1978.

The fall of the Soviet Union deprived Mugabe of a patron from whom he had expected steady income in return for permitting a Soviet stronghold in his country. It also deprived the WCC of an institutional embodiment for its theologies of liberation. Neither the country nor the council has fared well since the collapse of communism ended the Cold War.

Current conditions in Zimbabwe

The country's once-thriving economy is now in deep distress. Banks have failed. Farm land that once fed the native population and produced major exports lies fallow. The country's electrical and communication systems have fallen into disrepair and are now unreliable. Pickpockets freely roam city streets. Gangs slash the tires of tourists' cars at rest stops and rob drivers when they get out of their cars to repair the damage. Corruption fomented by Mugabe's appointees is blatant. (Because of a law passed by the party he controls, Mugabe himself is immune from prosecution.) The prices of basic commodities have risen 30 percent to 70 percent annually between 1991 and 1997. Inflation is so bad that Zimbabwean businesses – and even the government – often refuse payment for services in Zimbabwean dollars. Interest rates in 1997 soared more than 20 percent. According to government statistics, AIDS has infected more than 38 percent of the population, and there is only one public ambulance in the city of Harare, whose population exceeds 2 million. Mugabe's "land reform," a program to confiscate land from white farmers and return it to "indigenous peoples," has resulted in massive grants to Mugabe's friends and the creation of a land-wealthy class whose productivity is practically nil.

Current Conditions in the WCC

In developments that parallel Zimbabwe's misfortunes, the World Council of Churches has also fallen into hard times. The collapse of communist states, particularly East Germany, has dramatically diminished WCC income because WCC contributions from what was formerly West Germany, one of the largest WCC donors, are now staying home. Exposure by the popular television program, *Sixty Minutes*, and reports published by *Readers' Digest* that documented collusion between WCC officials and Soviet KGB agents during the Cold War have undermined the WCC's moral credibility. And mainline Protestant denominations in the United States, led by liberals who strongly supported the WCC, have felt their own financial pinch due to diminishing memberships and fewer discretionary dollars.

These losses have led WCC leaders to declare that some form of downsizing would be necessary if the organization is to survive beyond its 50th anniversary. Thus in this "Jubilee Celebration," WCC leaders discussed a "new ecumenical vision" that seeks to redefine what it means to be ecumenical in a pluralistic age. Some WCC leaders are advocating "macro-ecumenism," a term they use to welcome into the council's big tent groups who cannot affirm that Jesus Christ is the Son of God. The WCC, however, rejected this concept when it declared that it will formally associate only with groups that affirm Trinitarian faith.

The WCC concluded its meeting on December 14 with a giant "commitment" ceremony, an attempt to impress on member churches its need to find new cash for an otherwise collapsing ecumenical infrastructure. Whether representatives of those churches will be successful remains an open question. If the Presbyterian Church (USA) delegation in Harare is typical, denominational representatives who attended this event will sound a loud hurrah for the WCC's intentions. In large measure, the Presbyterian delegation is comprised of long-term WCC and COCU (Consultation on Church Union) supporters whose influence has led the Presbyterian Church (USA) to become the largest United States donor to the WCC.

But times are changing, even in the Presbyterian Church (USA). Leaders with a passion for the World Council of Churches are aging out of the Presbyterian system, and the new breed, while strongly ecumenical, tends to support *evangelical* ecumenism, a movement that WCC leaders long ago abandoned in favor of international politics. And so on this 50th anniversary of the WCC in Harare, two old allies have much to remember. They also have much to anticipate, for each faces a very different future than it could have anticipated when bullets and bombs punctuated their partnership. Robert Mugabe and the WCC discovered in Karl Marx a vision that served them both for a season. Neither has much to say about that any more.

But something must be said. And what more appropriate place to say it than in Zimbabwe, where it all began. If perchance these partners choose not to address such matters, then those of us who have witnessed what this association has done over the years must do so. It is not by accident that we all return to Zimbabwe.

This report was written en route to Harare, Zimbabwe.

The Layman Online

The Sept. 18, 1978, issue of *TIME* magazine called the downing of an Air Rhodesia Viscount airliner and murders of some of the crash survivors "a genuine horror story, calculated to make the most alarming of Rhodesian doomsday prophecies seem true."

The *TIME* report included vivid descriptions by crash survivors who hid in the bush while guerrillas murdered men, women and children with automatic gunfire.

"It's only because I know a terrorist when I see one that I'm still alive," Anthony Hill, then an Army reservist, told *TIME*.

'Please don't shoot us!'

"At first the guerrillas, clad in jungle green uniforms, seemed friendly, promising help," *TIME* reported. "But then they herded together the ten people at the wreckage, robbed them of their valuables and finally cut them down with automatic weapon fire. From another hiding place, businessman Hans Hansen and his wife Diana could hear the victims crying, 'Please don't shoot us!' as the firing began.

"Dazed by the ordeal, Hansen said later: 'I'll never be able to get that moment out of my mind.'"

The *TIME* report, titled "Seeds of Political Destruction," said that of the 56 people aboard the plane, 38 died in the crash. Five of the 18 survivors struggled free and left in search of water. Three of the remaining 13 survived by hiding in the bush.

TIME quoted Joshua Nkomo, co-leader of the Patriotic Front guerrillas, who received both moral and financial support from the World Council of Churches, as boasting that his men had shot down the plane but denying that they had murdered survivors.

C apitalism took a major hit at a meeting of the World Council of Churches when delegates enacted a resolution on international economics. Condemning "globalization," its term for free-market economies that invest capital in developing nations, the WCC said it would work for the establishment of "global governance" that will rein in the activities of transnational corporations, making them accountable to an international body. All eleven delegates of the Presbyterian Church (USA) voted for the resolution.

'Global predators' and income redistribution

"Globalization is devouring the earth," declared United Church of Canada Moderator William Phipps, who created an uproar in his own denomination last year when he granted an interview with *The Ottawa Citizen* and promptly denied the central doctrines of the Christian faith. In the interview and subsequent comments, Phipps denied the virgin birth, the bodily resurrection of Christ, the existence of heaven and hell, and, most directly, the deity of Christ.

Phipps told the WCC: "We need to be serious about redistributing income." Confessing that the headquarters of many corporations that conduct business on a worldwide scale are located in his territory, the United Church of Canada moderator said, "These global predators need to be held accountable ... Our people need a conversion experience ... and conversion has to do with economic relationships. Economic relationships are central to our understanding of the faith."

"If you would like to write that down in the form of an amendment," said Marion Best, a member of the WCC's Central Committee who stood at the podium, "I'm sure our committee would accept it." Best was also a delegate from the United Church of Canada.

'Global governance'

After discussing Phipps' ideas over lunch, Best's committee returned to the WCC business session with a revised globalization statement that reflected his passion for managed economies. "In view of the unaccountable power of transnational corporations and organizations who often operate around the world with impunity," said the revised statement, "we commit ourselves to working with others on creating effective institutions of global governance."

The statement called for an alternative to free-market economics: "The search for alternative options to the present economic system and the realization of effective political limitations and corrections to the process of globalization and its implications are urgently needed," it said.

Free-market economies denounced

In an appendix to its Polity Reference Committee Report, the WCC spelled out its condemnation of the free-market system. Reminding delegates that the WCC's support for liberation movements helped win victories for black revolutionaries over white colonial powers, the WCC document said that the battlefield had now turned from a military front to an economic front. The new war will be waged between the haves and the have-nots of the world: "Despite the independence of many formerly colonized peoples, power is increasingly concentrated in the hands of a relatively few nations and corporations, particularly in the north … Major decisions are made by these 30 or so nations and 60 giant corporations."

The WCC's statement is consistent with a theme that was promoted throughout this gathering on African soil, namely that the economic failure of many post-colonial economies is the fault of "the north," primarily the USA. Little attention has been paid to the fact that prior to WCC-supported wars of liberation, many of these countries not only produced food for their own people, but exported their products to countries all over the world. Now economies in these countries are failing, their infrastructure is crumbling, basic monetary, utility, social and health services are underfunded and unpredictable. But rather than acknowledging that many of these problems are due to governmental incompetence and corruption, the WCC has blamed free-market economic systems in "the north" for sucking the life out of Third-World countries.

The WCC's finances

Prior to its discussion of international economics, the WCC considered a report on its own financial condition. "From 1948 to 1998, the vision of the WCC has always been greater than its financial resources," said the opening sentence of its finance committee report. Huge operating deficits of approximately 13 million Swiss francs in 1994 and 12 million Swiss francs in 1995 forced the WCC to cut its staff from 340 to 237. The organization says it hopes to live within its income in 1999.

In addition to their operating budget crisis, WCC managers are reporting huge losses in their investment portfolio. In spite of the fact that most investors enjoyed the benefits of a bull market in 1997, WCC investment income dropped from 10,774,000 Swiss francs to 5,669,000 Swiss francs.

Authors of the financial report blamed the decline on "exchange rate fluctuations and some exceptional losses on transactions."

Income irony

Forty-eight percent of the WCC's member churches make no contribution to the organization's budget. That has led the WCC to say that it will try to get more money out of its member churches, imposing a requirement that all members make at least a minimum payment to the organization.

But the prognosis is gloomy. The WCC is highly dependent upon the very economies whose capitalistic ventures it has denounced as morally repugnant. Western Europe supplies 81.76 percent of the WCC's income, with most of it coming from Germany. The USA and Canada provide 15.83 percent. The rest of the world provides 2.41 percent of the WCC's income. The Presbyterian Church (USA) is the largest denominational contributor to the WCC in the United States. The PCUSA gave the WCC $1,799,386.77 in 1996, according to PCUSA officials.

The World Council of Churches *padare* (a Shona word for "meeting place") on gay and lesbian issues was conducted by two homosexual leaders who summarized their research on sexual orientation, recounted a sexual orientation history from the homosexual point of view, and divided the participants into small groups to share their gay/lesbian experiences.

The first to speak was a lesbian woman who said that she and two gay men had conducted "extensive research," inquiring whether gay and lesbian people could change their orientation. "After many months," she said, "we concluded that we couldn't find anyone whose orientation was actually changed." No information was shared on the researchers' sample or the questions asked by researchers. No statistical data were presented. Instead, the point was made that "unless we stop saying people can change, we can't get on with liberation. When gays and lesbians are diminished, all are diminished."

Homosexual history

Next a Norwegian gay man addressed the group on the history of homosexuality from the homosexual point of view. He said that homosexuality was an ancient phenomenon. "It was practiced openly in the Roman world," he said, "so early church leaders were well aware of it." Yet, he argued, their writings say very little about it, presumably because the subject was not a priority for them. The practice was widely accepted and no one made an issue of it.

The speaker said it was not until the Middle Ages that homosexual relations were called a sin. There were no marriages in the middle ages, he said, except among the upper classes where the institution was established in order to ensure the transfer of property. Later, the romantic era changed the foundation of marriage from economics to love, and in the industrial period, familial associations developed.

"In this situation," said the *padare* leader, "gays and lesbians came to see themselves as outlaws. But we learned to hide our lifestyle from heterosexuals, accept ourselves, and find community with others who shared our sexual orientation. These struggles finally led us to organize within our communities, and now gays and lesbians are coming out. We are here at the WCC today, not as persons on the outside looking in, but as people on the inside coming out."

Following these two speeches, participants were divided into small groups to "share our stories and our experiences of homosexuality in the church." One small group included representatives from Norway, Sweden, the Netherlands, Southern Italy, the United Kingdom and the USA. With one exception, all members of the group were homosexuals or they were heterosexuals who declared themselves strongly committed to the "normalization" of homosexuality in church and society.

Two Americans dominated the discussion. Robert E. Koenig, who identified himself as a Presbyterian/United Church of Christ minister, praised the pro-gay position of the UCC and confessed that Presbyterians "still have a lot of work to do." Bryan Grieves, an Episcopal minister from the USA, said he was "ashamed of what happened at Lambeth" when Anglican bishops from around the world issued a strong statement condemning homosexual activity.

Zimbabwean woman lifts up Scripture

After an extended period in which homosexuals in the group shared stories describing the pain of exclusion, Roselyn Manika, a Zimbabwean woman who had entered the circle carrying her Good News Bible, requested permission to speak. "I am very confused here. When I became a Christian I was taught that the Bible is the Word of God. I was taught to follow what the Bible teaches, and I want you to show me what the Bible says about this subject. How do you read the Bible and do all these things that you are talking about?"

Manika's question stopped the discussion cold. After extended silence, Grieves said, "We're not here to talk about that. I don't want to talk about it." A woman in the group who said she was "a lesbian in a partnership" said, "I don't know about the Bible, but this issue that we are here to discuss is a power issue. We have to discuss the dominance of heterosexuals ... their control of us. Why should heterosexuals tell us that their way is right?"

Man and woman together

But the woman from Zimabawe was not to be put off. "In the Bible, it is always man and woman together. Here, I open my Bible ... where do you find it different? Where does man and man, and woman and woman come from? Show me this in the Bible."

Koenig responded: "Obviously the Bible came out of a different time. The important thing that Jesus lifted up was that people should support one another."

"But here, look at this – how you say it? – Genesis," insisted Manika. "Here is Adam and here is Eve. God made them for each other. God did not make two men ..."

"I think you take this too literally," said Koenig, "You need to take into account the cultural context."

Who speaks for Africa?

A white male from the Netherlands suggested that the group not regard Manika as a true representative of Africa. "I think we need to be careful not to speak of all of Africa," he said. "After all, South Africa was the first country in the world to make same-sex marriages legal."

At this point the group turned to various psychological explanations for "heterosexism." Some suggested that it comes from "fear of the other." Others equated it with hatred. One woman identified herself as "a theologian who is interested in deconstructing human sexuality issues." She said she was trying to discover "the origin of the normativity of heterosexuality and then in deconstructing it." Koenig suggested that in light of the population explosion, there ought to be a greater appreciation of homosexuals. "Nowadays," said the Presbyterian/United Church of Christ minister, "homosexual relationships are to be preferred to heterosexual ones because they don't increase the population."

Scripture causes problems

Grieves returned to Manika's concern: "On this Bible question, I would hope that Scripture would not be used as a basis. That's a real concern that I have. The Bible can be used to support anything."

Koenig joined his Episcopal colleague: "He's right. The Bible is against usury. And that's the basis of the whole capitalist system."

At this point, *padare* leaders blew the whistle and their small groups were brought back together. There were testimonies as to how good it was to have this time of sharing feelings and experiencing one another's pain. "We are one small group in this assembly," said the lesbian leader, "and we want this issue to be brought into the agenda of the WCC."

A woman in the group identified herself as the WCC's "official listener," and she assured those present that their concerns would be presented at WCC hearings later in the week. Following that assurance, the *padare* was dismissed.

Indigenous peoples of the earth were told that "solidarity and self-determination" are their only hope in a world where Christians have stolen their spirituality, language and land.

Several WCC *padares* (a Shona word for "meeting place") focused on the plight of indigenous people. Like the African sun, indigenous anger rose to a searing level, matched only by the contrition that was confessed by white Westerners, many of whom wore African clothing, presumably to demonstrate their solidarity with the oppressed. In the WCC's first full day of *padares*, the rage/remorse syndrome assumed center stage.

Supporting the shamans

A *padare* on the Sami people, reindeer herders from the Arctic who are fighting Norway, Sweden and Finland for control of their land, started out as a geography lesson. Three *padare* leaders, dressed in brightly-colored costumes, talked about the history and culture of their people. They said they were being invaded by mining interests who, with the complicity of the Christian church, are pushing them north.

Anger accelerated as they told how Sami faith had been discounted by Christian missionaries in the past and is still demeaned by the Church today. "Our people have shamans," said a Sami leader. "When a women is pregnant, the shaman communes with the ancestors." Ancestors decide which of them will return to earth in this birth, and the woman names her child accordingly. Thus the shaman links two worlds.

This, said the *padare* leader, is "what missionaries took from our people." A woman in the group then said that when she tried to introduce a shaman element into her church's liturgy, leaders – whom she labeled "conservatives" – resisted. "They called it syncretism," she said.

A chorus of dismay rose from other indigenous people in the room, and a young man from Ghana jumped to his feet, raised his fist and yelled, "They did that to our witch doctors!"

"Me too," shouted a man from Bolivia.

"Come to the *padare* next door, and you'll hear more," said a Native American.

Beating the drum for justice

Titled "Spirit of the Land – Rhythm of the Drum," the *padare* next door had a distinct beat to it. Entering the room a few moments early, I saw a man with flowing black hair, sharply defined cheek bones – clearly

a North American Indian – playing a drum. Hoping to photograph him
before the session began, I extracted my camera from its bag and
attached the flash unit. By this time he had laid the drum on a table, so I
introduced myself and asked if he would hold the drum for a photograph.

"I cannot do that." he replied, "I don't know this drum."

"You don't actually have to play it," I responded. "I only want you
to hold it for the picture."

"But this is not my drum."

"Surely the owner won't mind if you just hold it for a picture," I
pleaded.

"The drum has feelings too. It has a life of its own."

Moving to the center of the room, the *padare* leader then announced
to a gathering crowd that it was entering Indian country. "You are now
on Indian land, and you will respect our traditions, something that the
white invader never did."

Beating the drum, the *padare* leader began to chant a prayer while
several fair-haired Americans wearing African garb closed their eyes and
swayed to the rhythm. Then, he torched a clump of sage and commenced
wafting smoke around the room with an eagle feather, a ritual called
smudging.

Litanies of oppression

At this point two women and a man entered the room. Scotch tape
sealed their lips. The leader smudged each of them from top to bottom
and sent them around the room to shake hands with WCC delegates.
"The handshake is very important to us," said the leader. "It means that
we now have a relationship that you cannot break. So you cannot leave
this room until we're through. This handshake was broken by the white
man. He stole our land and our spirituality which is intimately connected
with Mother Earth. You will not break this handshake."

Ceremoniously, the *padare* leader removed the tape from his
companions' lips, and for the next 45 minutes, they told "stories," a
litany of abuse and oppression that Native Americans have suffered. Two
white women in the audience, one who appeared to be American and the
other who was Swedish, became visibly disturbed and began making
sympathetic sounds. The *padare* leader punctuated those sighs with his
drum, provoking additional expressions of mounting outrage.

A woman from Turtle Island who identified herself as a United
Methodist leader said, "I was silenced by the church. I will be silenced
no longer. We are uniting with indigenous people around the world.

When we are on the land, we feel the spirits of our ancestors. How else could five pagans stand up against five million Christians? We have a different salvation plan, and it has to do with the land."

She named a long list of abuses that she and her people had suffered at the hands of white people, including criticism by church leaders over the fact that Indians are hosting gambling casinos on their land. "In our culture, we have always had games," she said.

Show and tell

A young man who identified himself as Richard Brown walked to the front of the room. Unwrapping his multi-colored blanket and lowering it to his groin, he asked, "What did you come here to see? I am naked. Here is my voice, and it is yet to be silenced." Brown's complaint focused primarily on his people's loss of their native tongue.

Visibly moved, an American woman cried out "Oh thank you, thank you. Thank you for not giving up on the rest of us. Thank you for teaching us. Thank you for giving us a chance …."

At this point a Peruvian man rushed forward. "We must unite," he said as the _padare_ leader pounded his drum. "The church cannot save us!" (another drum beat). "Let us search for an inter-religious dialogue that will give us solidarity." (More drum beats and applause).

One and a half hours after having smudged this gathering, the _padare_ leader summarized its visit to Indian land. "Indian people have been severely hurt for 500 years," he said. "But we know that if there is any healing, it must come from ourselves. It will not come from the church (drum beat). It will not come from the government (drum beat). It will not come from the white man (drum beat). It will come only from ourselves. You cannot heal us, but you can stand with us in our healing … and you can work for your own healing also."

A WCC program

This _padare_ was more than multi-cultural entertainment amidst a smorgasbord of seminar selections. It was designed to demonstrate an on-going program conducted by the WCC through its Justice, Peace, and Integrity of Creation division. The WCC's Indigenous People's Program claims that its purpose is "to clarify the past and present issues of denial, destruction and denigration of indigenous spiritualities and ancestral values ..." The program states its goal: "justice through indigenous sovereignty, repossession of their lands and a renewed call for a greater participation in the life of the member churches and the WCC itself."

Included in the WCC program are the objectives of obtaining for and with indigenous people "self-determination and autonomy" and "religious rights to develop their own spiritual life." WCC principles that form the program's content and direction include an explicit rejection of "the assumption that the Gospel/Bible culture [is] the only Good News." Consistent with that assumption, in more than three hours of *padare* discussion, Jesus Christ was never mentioned.

A t a World Council of Churches gathering titled "Evangelicals and the Ecumenical Movement," Mrs. Joyce Nima, a delegate to the WCC Assembly from the Anglican Church in Uganda, compared the WCC's Forum Plan to African women's experiences with polygamist husbands.

In an attempt to increase participation by groups that are not – and do not wish to be – members of the WCC, assembly officials proposed the WCC's sponsorship of forums, meetings where non-WCC members can gather and dialogue with representatives of the WCC. Ideas and proposals generated by such forums would be channeled into the WCC's program by WCC forum participants. The plan is designed to achieve participation without membership.

Avoiding accountability

But Nima sees flaws in the plan. She believes that it opens the door to associations that have no accountability. Pointing to tensions between the WCC leadership and Orthodox Christians, Nima says the WCC has not been able to get its own house in order. It should do the hard work of debating differences within its present family before it seeks to enter other, less accountable relationships, she said.

Comparing the Forum Plan to Africa's experience with polygamy, Nima said, "After a marriage of 50 years [the age of the WCC] the husband fails to get consensus in his homestead and he goes for a soft option. He marries another wife … but since he is the same, weak-willed coordinator, the problems of the first marriage will resurface as soon as the honeymoon is over."

Nima called on WCC leaders to turn away from their preoccupation with secular concerns, "go back to the foot of the cross, and see what the Bible has to say." She said that the forum idea was simply another way to accelerate the WCC's secular "globalization agenda" in lieu of concentrating on the organization's first love, the gospel of Jesus Christ.

Polygamy

Ironically, the illustration chosen by Nima appeared before the WCC Assembly two days later in a different context. The Celestial Church of Christ of Nigeria applied for membership in the WCC. During plenary discussions, it was disclosed that some members of the church's clergy engage in the practice of polygamy. That led Metropolitan Anba Bishoy of the Coptic Orthodox Church to move that the application be rejected. Membership was denied by a vote of 329 against, 234 in favor, with 57 abstentions.

Delegates who spoke in favor of admitting the Celestial Church argued that the taking of more than one wife is a long-standing African tradition that Christian missionaries – imposing their Western values on indigenous people – tried to destroy. Densen Mafinyani, general secretary of the Zimbabwe Council of Churches, said "We don't want our Christian faith to be limited by the mindset of Europe, where it came from." Mafinyani called the missionaries' faith and ethics "too narrow to accommodate what God has done with Africans long before the missionaries, who threw out our ancient religious experiences and sacred beliefs as pagan."

Mafinyani also said that he thought the very open African practice of polygamy was more honest than the practice of many non-African clergy who are married to one wife but keep a secret girlfriend on the side.

D iane Knippers, president of the Institute on Religion and Democracy, addressed a gathering at the World Council of Churches Assembly, making a plea for the persecuted church. "There are glaring omissions in the political and social agenda of the ecumenical movement, and one of the major omissions," said Knippers, "is its failure to stand up for the persecuted church." High on Knippers' prayer list are Christian people in Southern Sudan who suffer virulent forms of persecution at the hands of Islamic government officials. Inhabitants of entire villages are being systematically slaughtered. Children are killed in front of their parents. In areas of severe food shortages, Islamic government officials distribute food given by other countries only to persons who are willing to sever their ties with Christianity. In some areas Christians have been crucified.

Ignoring the evidence

In spite of overwhelming evidence documenting these crimes, the WCC has distanced itself from any public stance on behalf of Christians in Southern Sudan. "Officials from the WCC go to Khartoum and have conversations with the government of Sudan and don't address the situation of Christians there," Knippers said. "The WCC has a shameful record on this subject."

Knippers' words came into graphic focus when Mrs. Sarah Ajae Omot Obal, a member of the Presbyterian Church of the Sudan, appeared the following day at a hearing on "Peace, Justice, and the Integrity of Creation." Speaking in a gentle voice, her words came in stark contrast to soap-box tirades delivered by proponents of "gender rights." Describing the suffering of her people, she made no demands, and only one request. "Please pray for us," she asked.

Later that day, a special "crisis meeting" of delegates and visitors from Sudan called on the WCC Assembly not to be party to a conspiracy of silence on the genocide in Southern Sudan. A statement issued by Sudanese delegates and visitors at the conclusion of the meeting sharply criticized the WCC. "We ... are deeply disturbed by the lack of concern by the WCC on the issue of the Sudan conflict," the statement said.

Earlier in the assembly meeting, on Dec. 5, Bishop Paride Taban, Roman Catholic bishop of Torit, Sudan, made a special appeal to the WCC. Shortly thereafter, bombs were detonated in Narus, where the bishop's headquarters are located, killing six Nuer people and injuring 16 others. Unconfirmed reports say that the bombing attack was in retaliation for the bishop's appeal to the WCC.

Persecuted Christians in other areas of the world have also found the WCC silent in response to their plight. An open letter to the WCC from unregistered churches in China has received scant attention from WCC officials. Instead, WCC leaders invited representatives of the government-recognized China Christian Council to the Harare assembly where they were given a platform to represent Christians in their land.

Similarly, the WCC has honored the Korean Christian Federation, an organization recognized by the communist dictatorship of North Korea, and it has ignored the cries of unregistered Christians in the land who will not compromise their faith. The WCC has also waged a campaign intent on pressuring the United States to lift its embargo against Cuba, but it has failed publicly to recognize the plight of Christians whom the Castro regime has persecuted.

Knippers' warning that the WCC not repeat past mistakes refers to the fact that, following the fall of the Soviet Union, KGB records were discovered, documenting years of collaboration between WCC leaders and government officials who systematically persecuted Christians in Russia and Eastern Europe during the Cold War. Following an expose by *Readers' Digest* and CBS television's *Sixty Minutes*, WCC officials admitted that their support for persecuted Christians in Soviet-dominated Europe had been minimal.

Meanwhile, an interesting alliance has developed in the United States where, largely due to the work of Knippers' Institute on Religion and Democracy, the plight of the persecuted church has gained national attention. In contrast to the WCC's silence, Jewish communities have stepped forward on behalf of persecuted Christians. Remembering those Christians who endangered and, in many cases, sacrificed their lives to shelter, feed and rescue Jews during the holocaust, Jewish organizations are joining Christian groups who are crying out on behalf of the persecuted church.

Knippers says she traveled to Harare, believing that it is not too late for the WCC to take up this concern. She reminds those who will hear her that since persecutions under the Caesars in ancient Rome, Christians have protected, defended and sustained brothers and sisters who were under attack. She is calling on the WCC not to abandon Christians who are suffering and dying for their faith.

P reaching to an overflow crowd at Harare's Anglican Cathedral, Rt. Rev. George Carey, Archbishop of Canterbury, declared the words of Isaiah, "Let us go up to the mountain of the Lord." That journey, he said, will take the WCC directly to the throne of Jesus Christ, the center from which anything the WCC says or does must flow.

In a sermon titled "Crisis or Christ," Carey reminded the WCC that in the biblical sense, crisis is not a word of doom but a moment of decision. He challenged the WCC on its 50th anniversary "to seek unity in the service of Christian mission to the whole world." Carey said that if the organization grounds its work on any other basis than Christ's mission, it will sink.

Born in mission

Recalling that the WCC emerged from the worldwide missionary movement, Carey honored the organization and its founders. "In mission the church found its unity," he said. "But now there is a crisis," he said. "In some ways the splits [in the Christian community] are wider now. The Roman Catholic Church is still outside the WCC. The Orthodox are nervous about their continued participation in the WCC, the church in the West is in serious decline, and the future of the WCC is in doubt. This is a time, said Carey, for the WCC to remember that the only reason for its existence, and the only hope it has for continuing to exist, lies in Jesus Christ.

Jesus Christ the heartbeat

"The resurrection," said Carey, "is the heart of faith. We must confess with our lips that Jesus Christ is Lord ... We must place all that we do, all of our concerns, all of our ideals, all of our hopes in the context of our faith in Jesus Christ." Carey recognized that the WCC has chosen to confront many vexing issues, from homosexuality to the Third-World debt crisis. These issues, he said, "must not be the all to end all ... they must be addressed only in the light of the gospel and our determination to take the gospel everywhere. ... If there is no God, there is no final justice, no peace ... nothing beyond this life. Christ must be the heartbeat of our living, preaching, and work for justice and peace."

The worship service into which Carey was welcomed proved a fascinating blend of high church Anglican and drum-beating African traditions. Priests in gilded robes proceded along the center aisle swinging incense pots on the ends of sterling silver chains, while lively Shona voices transformed stone walls into sounding boards, accompanied by drums, rattles and gourds. African passion and Anglo precision contributed to a rich and colorful litany while, suspended above the chancel, a huge crucifix carved by African sculptor Job Kakana from a single piece of Jacaranda wood gave the worship area a focus that was as distinctly Christian as it was distinctly African. Wearing orange banners, black and white Zimbabwean ushers stood in pairs to assist their guests.

Sung by this multi-cultural congregation in Shona and English, the final hymn spoke to the power of the gospel to reach the very ends of the earth: "Jesus shall reign where'er the sun does his successive journeys run; His kingdom stretch from shore to shore, till moons shall wax and wane no more."

Although no vote was taken, and there seemed to be as many opinions about God as there were persons in the room, participants in the World Council of Churches *padare* titled "My God, Your God, Our God or No God" appeared to concur that "openness" and the avoidance of absolutes were the preeminent virtues to be pursued when encountering other faiths.

The 'absolute' implies no absolutes

The *padare* (a Shona word meaning "meeting place") commenced with a lecture by Anant Rambachan, a Hindu whom the WCC invited to lead its interfaith discussions. Seeking a starting point, Rambachan said that all religions reject materialism and affirm the existence of "an Absolute." This Absolute, said Rambachan, cannot be known, "for a God who can be known by finite persons would not be the Absolute." Thus, he suggested that various religions are, in essence, different languages that we humans use to speak of the Absolute, and that no statement should be "absolutized."

"I am a fellow traveler on a vast highway, interacting with others along the way. I am transformed by these interactions," said Rambachan. While God is One, he said, we each choose "a form of the One to be the center of our lives. We cannot be committed to all forms of the One, so we choose one form, while recognizing that forms others choose are also valid." Rambachan said that it is important for us to engage one another and build bonds of trust "so that all of us can know, not my God but our God."

Respondents represent their traditions

At the conclusion of Rambachan's lecture, the group heard respondents chosen by the WCC to represent various "faith traditions." Representing Judaism, Rabbi Jack Bemporand took a philosophical approach. He urged members of the group not to duck behind theological statements that affirm God as mystery, for this is "the method we use to avoid theological embarrassment." Bemporand said that "people of faith" must come up with criteria for determining "those aspects of God that we can talk about." He said he found philosophers like Hegel, Kant and Whitehead helpful.

Rachied Omar, a Muslim from South Africa, responded to the speaker by expressing his conviction that one cannot understand God without first understanding himself. "The antithesis of religious commitment," he declared, "is arrogance. Whatever you think God is,

God is beyond that." Therefore, he argued, in order to affirm the ultimate, you must affirm diversity by encountering others. "Dialogue is not an option," he concluded, "but a requirement."

A Presbyterian presence

Jay Rock, a Presbyterian from the United States and a staff member of the National Council of Churches, was chosen to give the Christian response. He said most Christians would agree that faith involves rejecting materialism and affirming the "spiritual search," but beyond that, Christians disagreed among themselves on just about everything. He said Christian tradition holds that we know God in Jesus, but he went on to say that none of our ideas about God are "complete." He argued that the Reformed Tradition – which he claimed to represent – was "always open to new understandings."

Rock suggested that the fact that all humans are made in the image of God means that "community is God-given." That is a place to begin the dialogue, he said. He told the group that Christians are not of one mind on whether Christ is the only way to God. He also said Christians are divided on the propriety of engaging in missions and evangelism. But he said that all Christians would probably agree that "we must be about reconciliation in the world. God calls us to be one people. How can we live any other way?"

A Christian correction

Rock's presentation of Christianity was countered by another participant later in the *padare*. Rev. Andrew Wingage, a professor at Selley Oaks College in Birmingham, England, and a member of the United Society for the Propagation of the Gospel, suggested that Rock's words had been a rather poor representation of Christian faith. "I find it a bit disconcerting," he said, "that the Christian speaker hardly mentioned Jesus Christ and did not mention the Trinity at all. We must start with Jesus Christ. Jesus Christ is God's gift of himself to the whole world. Contrary to what some may assume, Jesus Christ is inclusive, not exclusive. Yes, he is a scandal to some, but he is the essence of the gospel."

Rock's comments were followed by those of a Buddhist who appeared as firm in his convictions as the Presbyterian was pliable. "The Buddha is the only religious leader who did not claim to be other than a human being," he said. "All ideas and concepts are human endeavors.

There is no higher being that sits in judgment over humans. Mankind has the power to liberate himself from all bondage. If the Buddha is to be revered at all, it is because he discovered and showed us the pathway. He was so perfect in his humanness that he later was regarded by others as super human."

Growing in the faith

At this point an Anglican priest told the group that one of the young people in his church, whom he had trained 25 years ago, is now a Buddhist monk. "I am delighted that one of my parishioners became a Buddhist. That shows that he is growing," he declared. "There seems to be a need for many Christians to hear and believe that there is an Absolute they can trust in, something that will make them feel secure. That's creating an idol. People who do that are not growing."

A young man who identified himself as a Methodist from South Africa joined the Anglican's cause. "Religions are causing pain around the world," he said. "These tensions are real. We must move beyond dialogue and search for a new language where we can connect with one another. We must look at our faith traditions as portals of entry into a greater oneness."

A matter of words

A man from New Zealand challenged the idea that religious differences are merely differences in language. He noted that this assumption had been repeated often during the *padare*, and he said he did not believe it to be true because it did not deal with the question of what is real and what is not real. "We must question the language that each of us uses to see if there is any reality behind it," he said.

Professor Dawn DeVris, a delegate to the WCC Assembly from the Presbyterian Church (USA), asked Rambachan to further develop his statement that commitment to a particular faith tradition is not contradicted when one engages openly in interfaith dialogue. Rambachan responded, "the problem is not with one's commitment to one's tradition, but when one has negative views about other traditions. Each of us must each say that God is beyond our understanding before we can be open to interfaith dialogue."

The *padare's* closing comment was made by Rabbi Bemporad: "We have to start, not in our faith traditions, but our position as human beings. If you start in your tradition, then you're stuck. We cannot dialogue from there. We must begin in our humanity."

His Excellency Robert Mugabe, president of Zimbabwe, addressed the Eighth Assembly of the World Council of Churches with praise for its support in the revolution that brought his party into power. Remembering the 1969 Notting Hill conference where the WCC decided to fund Mugabe's Patriotic Front, the president said that this "courageous gesture" jolted the local church in Rhodesia which, he said, had "in effect sold its soul to the colonial Caesar."

"Today I present to you the country towards whose liberation you struggled, a free Zimbabwe, " said Mugabe to vigorous applause. "Zimbabwe thanks you, the World Council of Churches!"

Mugabe reflected on the diverse cultural composition of the WCC and recognized the Third World delegates who filled the Assembly hall. "Given this diversity and global representativeness, the United Nations, based as it is on dry political and international law principles that pay scant regard to spirituality and morality, must surely take full cognizance of you or otherwise face a real challenger."

'Ambiguous' experience

The president called Southern Africa's experience of Christianity "an ambiguous one," that encapsulates both "positive" and "warty" aspects." "The church lent holiness to one supposedly superior race and its high-handed, exclusionary structures of misgovernance," he said. "Indeed, as Africans, we were children of a lesser God, and we have in our history instances where religious leaders not just provided chaplains to the force of the empire builder, but actually accosted the imperial force to destroy African kingdoms and culture."

While acknowledging that they built schools in the bush, providing the only education available to his generation, and hospitals and clinics that still provide almost all the country's rural health care, Mugabe hammered hard on the evil that he said was committed by Christian missionaries. He said that most missionaries came as agents of the "empire builder" who paid them off with land and money "not for sound spiritual reasons, but to use religion as opium to take the indigenous population." Laced with fragments of the phrase first employed by Karl Marx, Mugabe's diatribe against Christian missionaries brought loud and sustained applause from this audience in which "indigenous" has been equated with holiness.

Mugabe pointed out that liberation struggles continue in many places around the world and that the Christian church continues to side with the oppressors. He spotlighted the Sandinistas in Nicaragua who, he said, had stood for the "most oppressed and marginalized and historically exploited."

Then Mugabe turned on capitalism and the scourge of debt that it has allegedly foisted upon Third-World countries. He lamented what has happened in the world since "the fall of communism," saying that the world is now a "heartless world dominated by bullies. It is a very conservative world where rich nations trample upon poor ones with disgusting impunity, a world where the widow still wails and the orphan still goes without."

Mugabe said it would appear that "there is a global conspiracy against our poor nations and poor people." He listed as evidence of the conspiracy the debt burden, unequal terms of trade, depressed commodity prices, speculative capital, and repeated droughts. All of this, he said, is the result of a "stupendous failure of the human system constructed for our so-called global village." And he asked, "Where is its conscience; where are ... our moral and spiritual liberators?"

Mugabe said that all Christians were not collaborators with evil. Some, he said, took the role of liberators who were willing to fight against colonial injustices. The WCC, he said, is representative of that kind of Christianity.

Revisiting communism

A former Marxist who was forced to modify his rhetoric when the Soviet Union fell, Mugabe appears to be returning to communist ideology. In his speech to the WCC, he bemoaned the rise of capitalism, blaming it for his country's post-liberation problems, and saying, "It is difficult to resist the temptation to conclude that perhaps our world would have been a lot better, a lot safer if we had given communism both a spiritual and democratic God than accept rampant capitalism as godly." At this point the assembly delivered its most enthusiastic applause.

Mugabe asked the WCC to help his government continue the struggle against vestiges of colonialism. Specifically, he requested support for his land reclamation policies which he described as returning the land to its people, and he asked that the WCC take on the issue of Third-World debt relief. "All we are saying is, can this great assembly of God find a heart for the underprivileged, landless peasant of Southern Africa?"

In stunning contrast to an almost reluctant reception given the dark-suited Robert Mugabe, Nelson Mandela, president of the Republic of South Africa received a tumultuous and joyful welcome, not only from delegates to the World Council of Churches, but also from thousands of Africans, leaping and racing through the streets as his motorcade entered the gates of the university.

Trim, informally dressed and greeting the crowd with a characteristically broad smile, Mandela appeared the picture of health. It was not until two assistants helped him mount six steps onto the stage that his frailty showed. But once behind the podium, with a voice strong and clear, he left no doubt who was in command. This crowd was putty in his hands.

Words of thanksgiving

With not one hint of recrimination and no mention of his 27-year imprisonment on a rock pile in the Indian Ocean, Mandela greeted his audience with words of thanksgiving. He recognized Christian missionaries who brought education, health care, and hope to his people. He thanked the World Council of Churches for helping to end apartheid and for respecting "the judgment of the oppressed as to what were the most appropriate means for attaining their freedom." He expressed his gratitude to the church for supplying the "noble ideals and values of religion" that he said are now embodied in his country's Constitution.

A marked contrast

There was a marked contrast between Mandela's speech and Mugabe's message on the previous day. Mugabe berated past foes; Mandela welcomed the future. Mugabe ascribed blame; Mandela envisioned partnerships. Mugabe demanded retribution; Mandela invited development. Mugabe lamented the fall of socialism and the rise of capitalism. He spoke of turning the tables and taking land away from whites. Mandela envisioned business opportunities for all and spoke of encouraging investors to enter the country and help build the new South Africa.

Mugabe represented a self-serving, one-party regime established and maintained by terrorists. Mandela expressed joy over the fact that there have been 40 democratic elections in Africa since 1990, and, with Mugabe sitting on the front row before him, he stated his hope that the people of this continent would "advance and entrench democracy, root out corruption and greed, and ensure respect for human rights."

There was a sense of finality to Mandela's words, a message that he believes he has done what he can for this land that he has loved. "It is a great privilege for me, as my public life draws to a close, to be allowed to share these thoughts and dreams for a better world with you," he said. "It is as a peaceful and equitable world takes shape that I and the legions across the globe who dedicated their lives in striving for better life for all, will be able to retire in contentment and at peace."

Then, in his final sentence, Mandela offered a summary of his speech.

"I thank you," he said.

The Rev. Clifton Kirkpatrick and Ms. Ashley Seaman have been elected to the Central Committee of the World Council of Churches. Kirkpatrick, who is stated clerk of the Presbyterian Church (USA), is one of the denomination's strongest supporters of the WCC. Seaman, a lay member of the Presbyterian Church (USA) delegation, is classified by the WCC as a youth delegate. During the Harare assembly, she headed a group that edited the WCC's position paper on peace in Jerusalem.

The constitution of the WCC grants broad powers to its Central Committee. Because the WCC Assembly meets only once every seven years, the 150-member Central Committee is, for all practical purposes, the WCC. That power was acknowledged during the assembly's opening session when Bishop Thomas Frederic Butler of the United Kingdom referred to it as the "Supreme Soviet" of the WCC.

The newly-elected Central Committee includes 39.4 percent women, 14.7 percent youth (persons under 30), 24.6 percent Orthodox, and 43.3 percent laypersons.

The nominating committee's first draft included 33 percent women, a statistic that brought United Church of Canada's Marion Best to her feet in protest. She told the assembly that in the light of their "Ecumenical Decade in Solidarity with Women," females in the assembly were expecting to do better than the 39 percent representation that they registered seven years ago in Canberra, Australia. She said that there are more women in the member churches than men and that the drop to 33 percent is "just unacceptable." Best threatened to walk out of the assembly if the nominating committee did not do something about the numbers.

The nominating committee scurried off and returned later with the winning slate that included 39.4 percent women. Best was unhappy that there had been only four tenths of a percent gain, but the figure was apparently encouraging enough for her to remain a part of the WCC.

The newly elected Central Committee members will serve until the Ninth Assembly of the WCC that is expected to take place in 2005.

lifton Kirkpatrick, stated clerk of the Presbyterian Church (USA), found himself staring down the throat of a giant hippo just days before the World Council of Churches opened its meeting in Zimbabwe.

Kirkpatrick and his son, David, had joined a canoeing expedition on a relatively calm section of the Zambezi River, just upstream from Victoria Falls. Cliff was in the stern of the canoe and David in the bow.

"We were the last canoe in the group," said Kirkpatrick who quickly discovered the painful reality that too much office work and too little exercise had diminished his fitness for the trip. "We were working hard just to keep up," he said.

As the flotilla rounded a bend in the Zambezi, the Kirkpatricks spotted several hippos along the bank. This was not the only wildlife they had seen in this hippo- and crocodile-populated section of the river basin, and it was no particular cause for alarm, because the distance between the main stream and the shore allowed a comfortable margin of safety.

"I noticed that the canoes ahead were moving around a big rock," said Kirkpatrick. But as he and David passed, some 25 feet away, the rock changed its shape dramatically. "It opened huge jaws, made a loud noise that sounded like an engine. Then it submerged and started after us."

Cliff said he and David paddled like never before. "It's amazing what you can do with a little motivation," he said. "Looking ahead, we saw an area of white water, and we headed straight for it." Kirkpatrick remembered a briefing in which they had been told that hippos don't like the rapids, so they reasoned that if they could beat the hippo into the turbulence, they might escape a more personal encounter.

"I was never so glad to see white water in all my life," said Kirkpatrick, who had been flipped out of his canoe in a stretch of rapids earlier in the trip.

The hippo experience apparently didn't dampen Kirkpatrick's enthusiasm for the Zambezi. A few days later he and David launched a rubber raft and ran the rapids in a canyon below Victoria Falls. "Our greatest challenge there was not the water, but climbing out of that canyon after the trip was over," he said.

Kirkpatrick said that after all that paddling, his hand and arm muscles were so sore that he had difficulty holding a pen to sign documents at the WCC registration desk.

W e as Christians need to help our government and the IMF (International Monetary Fund) to reflect on how they are asking these countries to pay their debt," declared Thelma Adair, a Presbyterian Church (USA) visitor to the World Council of Churches Assembly. Adair, a former Presbyterian Church (USA) moderator, was addressing members of the WCC press corps in support of a Third-World debt cancellation.

Poverty abounds

One does not have to travel far in this city to see evidence of the poverty that plagues its people. Taxi drivers said there were fewer beggars and street children than usual on Harare's streets, a result, they said, of police roundups that occur whenever a group like the WCC comes to town. "The police go around and collect them," said Joshua Mawindo, a driver who shuttled assembly visitors from the downtown hotels to their meeting site at the University of Zimbabwe. But despite such face-lifting efforts, evidence of the poverty that is crippling Zimbabwe abounds.

The economy is suffering its worst crisis since independence in 1980. Massive inflation that soars past 40 percent and a 70 percent drop in the value of the Zimbabwean dollar in the past 12 months have thrown this economy into turmoil. Hotels require payment in foreign currency. When merchants receive US dollars, they hoard them as long as they can, waiting for them to increase in value.

Blaming the West

Who is to blame for this crisis? President Robert Mugabe blames the rest of the world, primarily the West. He says that the "globalized economy" is destabilizing his country and that its $100-billion debt is crushing his people. Thelma Adair and a chorus of WCC regulars agree. Posters, rallies, T-shirt slogans, plenary speeches on the evil of "globalization," and feature articles in the assembly's official newspaper all promoted the theme that the Third World is poor because it has been victimized by the West. Debt cancellation was the suggested remedy.

But even in Harare, where the mass media is state-controlled, one can hear voices that challenge Mugabe's assessment of the problem. Professor John Mukumbe, reputed to be one of the country's most outspoken analysts, points an accusatory finger at Mugabe himself, and at the corruption that has riddled his government. Referring to government corruption, Mukumbe, who identifies himself as an evangelical Christian, told a correspondent to the WCC's Jubilee newspaper, "If the WCC does not understand the context of the country in which it is meeting, it is a sin."

Government corruption

The problem that arises in direct aid and loan programs is that donors and lenders have no assurance that money coming into the country accomplishes the purposes for which it was intended. International loans are channeled by government officials to corporations that are either unwilling or unable to develop the intended product. Company executives and government bureaucrats who are rewarded with kickbacks become wealthy and the Zimbabwean people end up saddled with further debt.

The debt continues to grow. Harare's major newspaper, *The Sunday Herald*, reported on December 6 that President Mugabe defied international sanctions by flying to Lybia where he negotiated a $100 million dollar loan (in US dollars) for the state's nearly bankrupt oil company from Colonel Moammar Khadafi. No details on the terms of the agreement were included in the report.

The newspaper also reported that Mugabe's wife, Grace, is on the list of persons identified in a scheme to defraud a home lending trust. According to the report, participants obtained $34 million in loans, ostensibly to build new homes or renovate old ones, and pocketed the money without applying it to housing. After being challenged publicly, the first lady repaid her loan of $5,848,333. Mugabe himself is immune from prosecution for any offense while he is in office.

Seeking a remedy

"Until something is done about government corruption, we will never get control of this problem," WCC delegate Timothy Royle told *The Presbyterian Layman*. Royle, a representative of the Church of England where he is a lay leader and a member of the General Synod, was a lonely voice in the Harare assembly. His complaint with the WCC was that it appeared to make public pronouncements on complex economic issues that reflected sentimentality in lieu of good sense.

"If world governments are going to listen to the WCC's counsel in such matters – and I must say that is highly unlikely – then we have to show that we understand the other side of the coin," said Royle. He proposed an amendment to the WCC's debt-cancellation proposal that would make some provision for dealing with government corruption.

"We have the same problems in the Church of England," says Royle, "where we make sweeping statements that have no relationship to the facts. The government just laughs at this. We simply must do a better job, and that's what I hope we can accomplish at this meeting of the WCC."

Sentimental economics

Frank Knaggs, another Church of England delegate, agrees with his colleague. He says he resents "accusations that we're bloodsuckers" when he and a handful of delegates suggest the need for fiscal and monetary controls. "WCC leaders think they are doing something for 'indigenous people, the poorest of the poor' when they promote these debt-relief proposals," he complained. "But that's emotion talking. They are not helping the poor at all. They are just lining the pockets of corrupt officials, and leaving the poor to repay the debt with taxes and inflation. And then we're told that we are actually responsible for getting them in debt, so we ought to forgive it for the sake of the poor."

Official resistance

Royle's amendment faced an uphill battle. During a press conference, a reporter asked WCC Moderator Aram I if he would be willing to entertain an amendment to the debt-relief proposals that would pressure Third-World governments on the issue of corruption. Aram dismissed the question, saying, "Corruption is everywhere." WCC General Secretary Konrad Raiser also responded, saying that it is "not the policy of the WCC to put pressure on governments."

When the issue finally reached the floor of the WCC, Royle's amendment survived, but not until a rider was added demanding that the debt be cancelled immediately, even if reforms specified in the amendment have not been accomplished.

At a private reception hosted at the State House in Harare for approximately one-tenth of the delegates to the World Council of Churches Assembly, President Robert Mugabe dismissed allegations of mismanagement, blamed his country's problems on a drought and unfavorable international prices for exports, and called for better church-state relations in order to build "a morally upright society."

Mugabe recognized the church as a mainstay of Zimbabwean society. He pointed to the fact that the country's school system was largely the product of Christian missionary endeavors and that several of his top government officials had experienced missionary education. The president also recognized the church's role in health care, acknowledging the fact that most hospitals in the rural areas belong to churches.

Mugabe thanked the WCC for holding its assembly in Zimbabwe, remarking that this conference was unique because it has a "spiritual dimension." Most conferences held here, he said, have dealt with "socio-economic issues.

In a formal reply to Mugabe, the WCC moderator, His Holiness Aram I, said he was happy to learn that the church in Zimbabwe was working together with the government. Countering the president's reference to the church's role in spiritual matters, Aram said the church was part of society and therefore it insisted on expressing its positions in the realm of politics.

ary Ann Lundy retired from her position as deputy general secretary of the World Council of Churches shortly after the WCC Assembly adjourned its meeting in Harare. The announcement of her retirement was made, not by Lundy, but by Rev. Clifton Kirkpatrick, stated clerk of the Presbyterian Church (USA), during a dinner for 130 Presbyterians who attended the WCC event.

Kirkpatrick expressed his delight at the large representation of Presbyterians at the WCC Assembly, calling it "a demonstration of our commitment to ecumenism." Not all Presbyterians were voting delegates. Several, many of whom are Presbyterian Church (USA) staff members, were titled "co-opted WCC staff," individuals loaned to the WCC and named as WCC staff members for the duration of the assembly. Others were labeled "Observers" and "Advisors," titles that the WCC gives to persons assumed to have a particular expertise or association that WCC officials deem useful to their assembly proceedings.

Another group of representatives is known as "Accredited Press." This category included staff persons of various news groups, such as the Presbyterian News Service and *The Presbyterian Layman*. It was another niche in which PCUSA staff persons have gained official status at the assembly by finding a cooperative periodical to designate them as reporters. Theodore Gill, who has served as denominational staff in ecumenical concerns like the Consultation on Church Union (COCU), came with reporter credentials from *The Presbyterian Outlook*. The WCC also had a category called "Visitors" that allowed persons to attend all assembly sessions, hearings and *padares*, informal seminars on selected topics.

Who represents the Presbyterian Church (USA)?

Large in number, Presbyterians at this assembly were heavily slanted in favor of those who do not represent the beliefs and values of the Presbyterian Church (USA) membership. Abundantly represented in the gathering were staff and elected leaders who have been most vocal in their support of liberation theology, a Marxist ideology expressed in theological language, and who have vigorously opposed the denomination's ordination standards relating to sexual behavior.

Two events, the fall of the Soviet Union and the 2-1 declaration of Presbyterian Church (USA) presbyteries confirming their constitution's ordination standards, have resulted in serious setbacks for these Presbyterian leaders in their own country. But here in Zimbabwe, where leaders from more than 100 churches around the world were gathered, the face of the Presbyterian Church (USA) were being represented by these individuals and the ideologies they espouse.

Apologists for Marxism

Included among those present were staff and elected leaders who supported the Marxist Ortega regime in Nicaragua until it was rejected by the Nicaraguan people in popular elections; channeled support to rebel forces in El Salvador in the name of "peace and justice;" oppose the United States embargo against the Castro regime in Cuba, and demonstrated against the US military buildup that stopped Soviet expansionism during the 1960s and 1970s.

ReImagining God

Also present were representatives of the Women's Ministry Unit, Presbyterian Women, *Horizons Magazine* and the National Network of Presbyterian College Women, many of whom attended and supported the 1993 ReImagining conference whose rejection of Scripture's teaching on the person and work of Jesus Christ was declared "beyond the boundaries" of Christian faith by the 1994 General Assembly.

Based on the ideologies expressed by most Presbyterians who gathered in Harare, world church leaders would have no idea where the Presbyterian Church (USA) stands on the issue of human sexuality. That was made clear during introductions at the denomination's dinner when a young woman representing the National Network of Presbyterian College Women stood to an enthusiastic and sustained applause. NNPCW is currently undergoing evaluation following discoveries that its resources and program encourage lesbian behavior on college campuses and promote theologians who deny God's transcendence and the atoning work of Jesus Christ. Those themes were highly visible in Harare where celebrations of the WCC's Ecumenical Decade of Solidarity with Women, a sponsor of the 1993 ReImagining Conference, have been given center stage.

Lundy declared 'PCUSA missionary'

The ideological slant of this group was made even clearer when Kirkpatrick singled out Lundy for special recognition. Kirkpatrick prefaced his remarks by saying that the greatest ecumenical challenge in the Presbyterian Church today is found among its own members. He urged members of his audience to work harder at winning greater appreciation for the WCC throughout the denomination. He expressed his opinion that those Presbyterians who serve as staff members in ecumenical agencies like the World Council of Churches do not receive the appreciation that they are due. "They are really our staff," said Kirkpatrick. "They work for us. They are PCUSA missionaries in the ecumenical movement."

Kirkpatrick said no one fits that description more aptly than Lundy who, he said, would "retire soon from her position with the World Council." He said that he believed he was speaking for many Presbyterians when he expressed to his good friend profound gratitude for her service to the denomination and the worldwide church. Kirkpatrick's words prompted a standing ovation.

Being 'fired up'

Lundy, who held several high-ranking staff positions in the James Brown administration of the General Assembly Council, was a key leader in the 1993 ReImagining Conference. Her efforts resulted in channeling a $66,000 Bicentennial Fund grant into the event. When the content of the conference became known, denominationwide outrage resulted in massive financial losses to the national church budget and Lundy's firing on the eve of the 1994 General Assembly, when it was clear that many congregations were ready to leave the denomination.

Shortly after she was fired, Lundy was named deputy general secretary of the World Council of Churches. At the "ReImagining Revival" in 1998, Lundy quipped that she had been "fired up." During her years at the World Council office in Geneva, Lundy promoted a broadened definition of ecumenism that includes organizations and movements that do not affirm Jesus Christ as Lord.

His Holiness Aram I, moderator of the World Council of Churches and a delegate from the Armenian Orthodox Church, highlighted deteriorating relations between the Council and the Orthodox community during his December 4 address to the assembly. Aram said the situation is "critical" and that unless problems are taken seriously, "Orthodox participation will steadily dwindle."

At issue for the Orthodox churches is the fact that they represent a minority voice (approximately 25 percent) in an organization that is dominated by Protestant liberals. The Orthodox take issue with WCC leaders' proclivity to embrace sexual behavior that Scripture calls sin, and they are offended by "evangelistic" visits into their countries by some member churches in the WCC. Referring to resignations from the WCC and refusals to participate as voting delegates at the Harare assembly, Aram said, "Some of our member Orthodox Churches are not with us in this assembly. Others are not with us the way they used to be. I am sure that we all realize that there is a problem, and that this is not an Orthodox problem but essentially an ecumenical problem."

Human rights

Another concern raised by Aram is the issue of human rights. "Human rights are integral to ecumenical witness," he said. Aram praised the Universal Declaration of Human Rights, adopted in 1948, the same year the WCC was founded, but he expressed regret that the UN has "proved its weakness" in redressing human rights violations. He said that in his opinion, the WCC had done a good job in condemning human rights violations, but it must do more to prevent them. This will require, said Aram, that the WCC take into consideration the effects of globalization, religious freedom, and ethno-nationalism on human rights.

Religious pluralism

The future of the ecumenical movement will, of necessity, be different from its past, said the Orthodox leader. Christian communities are having to learn how to deal with religious pluralism, and the WCC must help them dialogue with people of other faiths, he said. Aram suggested that materials arising from the WCC-sponsored Gospel and Culture Study might be helpful in this regard.

"Institutional ecumenism is in crisis," said Aram. "Much of our constituency is disillusioned with the institutional expressions of the ecumenical movement ... They are longing for fresh air to breathe and wider space to live and to express their ecumenical concerns and convictions." Aram said that unless the ecumenical movement shifts its approach from structures to "visions relevant to the life of the people" it could lose its vitality.

The Ecumenical Decade

Aram noted the fact that the WCC's Ecumenical Decade of Churches in Solidarity with Women was coming to an end. He said that the intention of this effort had been to make "each church, and indeed each congregation, into a truly inclusive community," and he expressed regret that "the churches have not been as responsive as was hoped." The Ecumenical Decade program has come under criticism for incorporating into women's liberation themes ideologies that deny Scripture's teaching on the person and work of Jesus Christ. He did give the program credit for having gotten more women ecumenically organized and helping them to find a voice for their frustrations and concerns.

Dwindling financial resources

Aram called for a sober look at financial realities facing the WCC. Noting that the organization has been told by churches of the "North and West" that "past levels of activity funding could not be sustained in the future," he called for the WCC to develop its investment and real estate revenues, seek higher contribution levels from churches in the Far East, and tighten controls on expenditures.

Aram concluded his speech declaring that the Jubilee Assembly called for a new commitment whose essence is, "We intend to stay together." He said that neither lack of progress, nor setbacks, failures, uncertainties, fears nor threats would weaken the WCC's intention to "walk together on the way to unity."

Acting Zimbabwean President Muzenda publicly thanked the
World Council of Churches for supporting the liberation war that
placed the Robert Mugabe regime in power. In a keynote address
on the assembly's December 3 opening session, Muzenda said the WCC
has been "a shining example of matching its words with action."

Muzenda expressed regret that Mugabe, who was in London, could
not bring personal greetings. Mugabe, an outspoken opponent of
homosexual activity, which is illegal in Zimbabwe, stated his displeasure
with the WCC's plan to allow gay and lesbian issues a platform during
the assembly. Spokesmen for the president indicated earlier that in light
of the WCC's intention to showcase this subject, Mugabe might choose
not to greet the assembly. But at a press conference, John Newbury,
WCC information officer, announced that Mugabe would speak the next
day.

Who owns the land?

Muzenda thanked the WCC for its partnership in Zimbabwean
development, and he called for Christians around the world to support his
government's controversial land reform, which he admitted is "not
without problems." Citing passages from Leviticus and Joel, Muzenda
said that the Bible clearly supports taking the land away from whites and
returning it to blacks whom he called "its rightful owners." Muzenda said
"Christians who came from the north with the mission of enlightening
the heathens" were responsible for the maldistribution of African land.

Government officials claim they are purchasing land from white
farmers and redistributing it among the landless poor. The program is
falling under heavy criticism due to the fact that the government pays a
fraction of what the whites – supported by independent appraisals –
believe the land is worth. Although some confiscated farm land has been
passed on to the poor, government officials' family members, friends and
business associates have acquired much of the property for themselves.
Even Harare's government-censored newspaper, *The Herald*, has cited
evidence that the program is resulting in a new class of wealthy blacks to
replace the class of wealthy whites.

On December 2, *The Herald* reported that a national people's
conference of the ruling party would be held later that month in Gweru to

focus on the land redistribution issue. About 5,000 party members were expected to address the growing problem of landless peasants invading farms because, according to *The Herald*, "Government had taken long to distribute land."

A Harare taxi driver, who asked that his name not be printed, told *The Presbyterian Layman* that in his observation, the Zimbabwean people are no better off now than they were before the revolution. He said he had supported the war of liberation in the hope that it would result in benefits for all the people, but now, he said, "my hopes are gone." Government officials and their friends are amassing great wealth while the poor are poorer than ever due to inflation (currently 35 percent and expected to reach 40 by the end of the year) and a poorly administered and rapidly deteriorating infrastructure.

Failures in the government-controlled Zimbabwean economy are numerous. The National Oil Company of Zimbabwe posted a huge loss of $1.7 billion in 1997 and prices at the gas pumps have doubled in recent months, causing "stayaways" by taxi drivers and the inability of low-income workers to pay bus fares. The Zimbabwe Iron and Steel Company has failed to meet targeted production levels due to obsolete plant and equipment and low sales against high expenditures. The company is reporting losses of $445 million. The National Railways of Zimbabwe recorded a $241 million loss, and the national airline, Air Zimbabwe, showed losses of $172 million.

On December 2, the day before the WCC's opening session, Harare headlines reported that one of the city's major hospitals, Parirenyata, had run out of blood. When the hospital's outstanding balance to the blood bank reached $2.7 million, blood bank officials cut off the supply. Patients are now told that they must pay up to $1,660 in advance for every unit needed or else they cannot be treated at the hospital.

Sounding the 'Jubilee' theme

Avoiding any suggestion that governmental corruption and incompetence might have contributed to Zimbabwe's problems, Muzenda expressed an opinion – common among WCC leaders – that Third-World economic crises such as those experienced by Zimbabwe were caused by the West. He stated his gratitude for the fact that WCC officials have placed "Jubilee debt relief" high on the assembly's agenda, referring to proposals that the United States, the World Bank and the International Monetary Fund cancel debts incurred by Third-World countries.

During an informal discussion after Muzenda's speech, the issue of corruption by Third-World leaders was voiced by Rev. Timothy Royle, a representative of the Church of England. Royle cited situations in which development loans are made through a Third-World government to businesses that have "no real means or intent of production." Royle said the real cost of such loans ends up on the backs of the people. "We must make a commotion about corruption," he said.

Similar concerns were raised by a German reporter at a press conference with WCC Moderator Aram I and General Secretary Konrad Raiser. Referring to WCC proposals calling for debt-relief, the reporter asked the WCC leaders to what extent they would pressure African governments to reform corrupt practices. Aram dismissed the question, saying, "Corruption is everywhere, not just in Africa." Raiser said that the WCC had no authority to put pressure on governments.

Reflecting Muzenda's theme that governments of the West are responsible for economic miseries currently experienced in Africa, assembly participant Tafadzwa Chigwedere said, "Governments around the world are looting the future of young Africans." Chigwedere, 23, who would later make a presentation on the subject of economics to the assembly, continued: "The problem of debt is painful to us ... Even if our debts are canceled, the West must stop trying to control African countries' economies." Chigwedere expressed disdain for World Bank and International Monetary Fund policies that have imposed fiscal and monetary control requirements on Third-World governments when they seek increases in their indebtedness.

ifty years ago, in August, 1948, 350 Christians from 147 churches in 40 countries gathered in the city of Amsterdam to forge a truly remarkable alliance. Emerging from the rubble of a worldwide war, they came with hope in their hearts. Inspired by their first love, they named Jesus Christ the one Lord who transcends every lesser loyalty. In that corporate confession, the World Council of Churches was born.

To whom shall we go?

In Europe, Africa and Asia – on every shore – memorials to men and women who had been struck down in their youth told a horrible tale. Craters where cathedrals once stood, tombstones aligned as far as the eye could see, proved our capacity – yes, even our propensity – to do inhuman things. The war had brought us to our knees. We had been forced to face graphic and heart-rending evidence that sin means nothing less than death. Counterfeit saviors had done us in. Masses once mesmerized by utopian ambition suffered the ruinous result of human pretension. We were left with one question and one answer, "Lord, to whom shall we go? You have the words of eternal life." (John6:68)

In that post-war moment, a commitment to Jesus Christ was reborn. Christians were seized with a passion for the gospel. Churches grew. Mission societies dispatched evangelists to faraway places. Scripture was translated into many languages.

Evangelism and ecumenism

Out there on the front lines, in places that had never heard the gospel, mission workers who called themselves Methodists and Presbyterians, Lutherans, Episcopalians, Baptists and others found that the person who united them was stronger than the differences that divided them. Jesus Christ, Son of God, Savior of the whole world, had made them one. *Oikoumene*, "the whole inhabited earth," was the word that came to the fore in Amsterdam. The mission imperative to proclaim the gospel throughout all the earth inevitably makes us *oikoumene*, ecumenical.

Amsterdam gave expression to the fact that the evangelical movement and the ecumenical movement go hand in hand. Proclaiming the name of Jesus Christ, a centrifugal thrust, also means coming together in Jesus Christ, a centripetal thrust. The more vigorously we move outward with the gospel, the more we find ourselves moving toward one another.

But the Amsterdam assembly realized that while sending forth the gospel is a Christian imperative, receiving it from those to whom it has been sent is no less so. In birthing the World Council of Churches they declared that Christian faith must not suffer cultural isolation. It is both in giving the faith and in receiving the faith from those to whom it has been given that our experience of Jesus Christ comes full circle.

Bishop Lesslie Newbigin, a principal founder of the World Council of Churches, saw the necessity of this cross-cultural exchange. Jesus Christ was not an amorphous, disembodied concept, Newbigin explained. "Jesus Christ was the incarnate one, God's self expression in the life of a particular human being who inhabited a particular culture, spoke a particular language, embodied a particular tradition."

And so he is today. With each new convert, the gospel finds a home in a unique cultural personality. The missionary whom we dispatch to another land cannot be divorced from his or her own language, traditions, affinities and values. And when the gospel takes root in a person of another culture, although the eternal reality of Jesus Christ, Son of God, does not change, the convert receives this Christ through his or her own unique set of filters and will now articulate that gospel in a language quite different from the one in which it was received. Thus the gospel finds its fullest expression when mission-sending cultures also become mission-receiving cultures. It is in this gospel exchange, this fellowship, this *koinonia*, that each of us is enriched by a gospel that has become embodied in another person.

The Amsterdam assembly declared, "The World Council of Churches is a fellowship of churches which confess the Lord Jesus Christ as God and Saviour according to the Scriptures, and therefore seek to fulfill together their common calling to the glory of the one God, Father, Son and Holy Spirit."

Those 350 Christians who gathered in Amsterdam affirmed a unity of faith amidst their diversity of cultures. They had no intention of becoming a mere society of religious ideas. What Scripture says about "the Lord Jesus Christ as God and Saviour" would be the content of their corporate confession. Thus Jesus Christ would be no mere product of human imagination, but the historical person to whom Scripture attests. Thus Jesus Christ would not be a mascot, some imaginative icon applied to a multiplicity of humanly-conceived ideologies. Confessing the Jesus

Christ whose life, death and resurrection are recorded in Scripture would form the basis of the World Council's unity.

The Amsterdam assembly understood that unity is a gift, not an accomplishment. It is the result, not the goal of Christian faith. The World Council of Churches would be an expression of that unity which Jesus Christ gives to all who follow him. It would be a "fellowship" of churches which – each in its own cultural particularity – confess "one Lord, one faith, one baptism, one God and Father of us all."

Fifty years later

The world has taken several turns since 1948, and we must now assess the current council's faithfulness to Amsterdam's vision. Forced to undergo restructure by diminishing financial resources, the council will consider a new statement of its nature and purpose when it meets in Harare, Zimbabwe. Inevitably, those who gather there must answer the question that was addressed by their predecessors fifty years ago: What is the basis of our unity?

Secular visions of world order had taken their toll when the Amsterdam assembly addressed that question, and commissioners were in no mood to encourage additional ideological aspirations. Instead, they turned to the only one capable of making all things new, and they found a basis for their unity in the Lord Jesus Christ. The discovery that they made on that occasion is no less valid today, "for there is no other name under heaven given among men by which we must be saved." (Acts 9.10)

Parker Williamson made these comments during an address to the National Press Club in Washington, D.C., on November 9, 1998. His remarks were included in a presentation by the Association of Church Renewal, whose representatives later attended the World Council of Churches Assembly in Harare, Zimbabwe, where they encouraged Christians to make an evangelical witness at the assembly.

F arming in any country is no picnic, but under a one-party dictator determined to eliminate every vestige of colonialism, white farmers in Zimbabwe face enormous odds. Because the heart of this country's economy is rooted in the land, this contest is no private affair.

Mary and Jim Oxford (whose names are pseudonyms) are third-generation Zimbabweans. "We've never lived anywhere else," he says, "so when government officials tell us to go home, where do they expect us to go?"

Loving the land

Carved out of the rich Zimbabwean soil, the Oxfords' farm reflects their love of the land. Contours are carefully terraced to prevent erosion by fierce African storms. Crops are rotated to ensure that nutrients remain in the soil. Cattle are moved from one pasture to another, and grazing areas are systematically re-seeded. Irrigation waters many hectares of citrus trees during the dry season.

The Oxfords made the brick that shaped their home. "We dug the clay out of ant hills," says Jim, "because ants remove the sand and we get better bricks that way." Mary's tiny flower garden receives superlative care. "I love my flowers," she says, "They remind me of God's goodness and this bountiful earth. When we treat the land with care, God rewards us with beauty."

Farm dependents

Dozens of black people live on the Oxfords' farm. In addition to being paid the minimum wage – a government requirement – workers are given incentive bonuses and land for their own gardens. Years ago, Jim's parents built a school for area children on farm property, and teachers are paid from farm income. Jim and Mary purchase medicine and provide medical care for all of their employees and their families. "It's the only health care available," says Jim. "The nearest clinic is a long way from here, and there's no public transportation."

Nothing comes easily for a Zimbabwean farmer. Mechanical parts are hard to find. If equipment breaks down, one had better be able to fix it, or find another way to get the work done. This is a pioneering kind of life. "If you break your leg, you're going to need to set it yourself. If the black mamba strikes, just say your prayers. You're going to be dead before help can arrive."

Hard work and sweat equity over several generations have paid off, not only for the Oxfords, but for hundreds of others who share the benefits of their harvest. A ready market for their crops has produced cash to cover their costs, money for investing in additional enterprises, and savings for the lean years that they know will come.

"Lots of people depend on our success," says Mary, who keeps the books for the farm operation. Zimbabwe has one of the highest tax rates on the African continent. The Oxfords pay sales tax, a fifty-percent income tax, property taxes and inventory taxes. They pay road maintenance taxes that government officials use as personal income, while their roads deteriorate from neglect. And they pay a social security-type tax on each worker which, like the road tax, disappears into the bureaucracy.

Reverse racism

When President Mugabe – he prefers the title "Comrade" – came into power, he promised land redistribution for millions of Zimbabwean blacks. The Oxfords were not opposed to that idea. "There is not a white farmer out here who doesn't understand the need for land redistribution," says Jim. "The government is sitting on millions of hectares of unused land. And there are millions more in the hands of absentee owners, people from other countries who own it and are doing nothing with it. This is the land that should be divided among people who have none. It is good land, and with proper care, it can produce."

But that's not what Mugabe has in mind. He is apparently after land such as that owned by the Oxfords, productive farms that have been developed and tended over the years. Several of these farms have been confiscated and given to Mugabe's friends and government officials. Precious few have been divided among the landless poor.

Land abuse

The problem with simply turning over farmland to Zimbabwean blacks lies in the fact that they must overcome huge cultural differences to make the land productive. The idea of investing is foreign to the African tribal mindset. These Zimbabweans come from nomadic ancestral stock who measured their wealth by the number of cattle they owned. Their practice was to move into a grassland area and graze it until there was nothing left. Then they moved on, assuming that Africa offered a limitless supply. This tendency to use whatever you can get today with no thought of what will be needed tomorrow is the death knell to farming.

In areas where the Zimbabwean government has resettled landless blacks, the land has suffered. Farms that had been productivity showplaces have stopped producing anything more than subsistence crops. Grass lands have been overgrazed. The new occupants have allowed erosion to wash away precious top soil. Once fertile maize fields are now ribbed with deep gullies and exposed rock. Having failed at their resettlement efforts, many occupants are simply moving away, now that the land can no longer sustain them.

Mugabe has apparently learned nothing from these results. *TIME* magazine reported that on November 28, 1997, with his aim set on 1,503 productive farms like the one owned by the Oxfords, Mugabe declared, "The colonial exercise of robbery will be corrected once and for all." Writing for *TIME*, author Remer Tyson reported, "Zimbabwe's white farmers, who produce 40 percent of all exports and employ 337,000 black workers, are shell shocked."

Religious rhetoric

The Oxfords had been reading reports of the World Council of Churches meeting in Harare, and they were baffled by the rhetoric. "They seem to be accepting Mugabe's lies," said Jim. "Mugabe told them that the country's economic problems are due to colonialism. How long is he going to blame the failures of his government on something that ended 18 years ago? This country was a lot better off before Independence. Just ask anyone. Everything here is falling apart. The roads are crumbling. Telephones don't work. We have power failures every day. Inflation is almost 40 percent. It is getting harder and harder to live in Zimbabwe, and the poor are suffering most of all."

The Oxfords are particularly incensed over WCC resolutions that romanticize "indigenous people," call for canceling Third-World debt, and propose a "global governance" that will curtail investments by transnational corporations. "If Zimbabwe's debt is canceled, don't expect the people, especially the poor, to benefit," says Jim. "Mugabe and his friends will pocket that money ... And making it harder for corporations to invest in our country is just shooting ourselves in the foot."

The WCC resolution does call for an end to government corruption in Third-World countries and the establishment of controls by creditors in any future loans. But it also says that cancellation of the debt should not wait until those controls are enacted.

No strangers to adversity, most white Zimbabwean farmers are tough, and they will not just walk away from this land that they have loved. But with eviction a distinct possibility, they may not have a choice. They are beginning to feel like an endangered species, and they don't see how resolutions from the World Council of Churches will make their lives any easier.

S ome beg; some steal. They do whatever it takes to survive on the streets of Harare. How did they get here? Many are orphaned in this city where, according to government statistics, 38 percent of the population is AIDS infected. Some come from drought-stricken Masvingo where there is no food, and children are abandoned to forage for themselves. Many have no idea why they came, and even fewer thoughts as to where they might go.

These are children adrift, wandering the streets, selling stolen trinkets and sexual favors to pay for food. Darting in and out of shopkeepers' stalls, they elude police who corral them like cattle, pack them into disease-ridden cells, and then disperse them onto a bleak countryside when the jails cannot hold any more.

'The least of these'

When Jesus spoke of caring for "the least of these," surely he must have had Harare's little ones in mind. That's what Gilbert Chikuni and Maury Mendenhall believe. Associates of Presbyterian missionary Nancy Warlick, Chikuni and Mendenhall operate Lovemore House, an oasis in the heart of Harare where children who once had no hope can find their way into the presence of Jesus Christ.

Chikuni, who was working for World Vision while attending school, ran into Warlick on the University of Zimbabwe campus. Mendenhall, now a volunteer-in-mission, met Warlick in the United States. Neither could resist her when Warlick wooed them into sharing her dream of a Presbyterian children's ministry in the capital of this desperately-poor country.

Chikuni and Mendenhall gather their hapless brood from a shelter in the city and a street children's program at City Presbyterian Church. "From the start, we involve the children in all of the decisions we make at Lovemore House," says Chikuni. "We do not force them to stay here, and if they run away, we have to let them do that. They must choose to live here."

Running away

Some children do run away. At Lovemore house there are rules and chores, restrictions that many of its residents had never experienced. They must clean their rooms, make up the beds, assist in the kitchen, study their school lessons and perform numerous tasks for the good of the house.

Authority takes on an entirely different meaning here. On the streets, it wore a uniform and was to be avoided. But there is an authority at Lovemore House that they must learn to accept. Here they are held accountable for the decisions they make and the things they do. They forfeit street freedom when they enter this community, learning, over time, that street freedom is no freedom at all. But for some – despite Lovemore's benefits – that lesson does not come easily.

If a child who has run away asks to re-enter the house, each resident must participate in the decision to take him back. "It is important," says Chikuni, "that we decide this together." He points out that not only do such discussions help to create a sense of community, they have a very practical effect. "If Maury and I decided to take someone back and the children did not accept him, that would never work," he says. "In reality, they do decide."

Connecting with home

Lovemore House is not a permanent arrangement. The policy calls for a tenure of no more than two years. So immediately upon receiving a child, Chikuni and Mendenhall begin working toward re-entry into the community that the child left for life on the street. In many cases, the parents are dead, and the extended family is not initially enthusiastic about taking in another mouth to feed. So the persistent Presbyterians and their foster child work together to show the family that this child is worthy of their acceptance and affection.

When Denis, age 14, came to Lovemore House, both parents were dead. Having been on the streets for many months, Denis was a well-known thief. When Chikuni finally located Denis' grandfather, the response was hardly jubilant: "We thought he was dead," said the grandfather. Undoubtedly one of Denis' victims, the grandfather was in no mood to discuss taking the boy back. But while working with Denis' at Lovemore, Chikuni continued to visit the old man. "He is a good, strong, hardworking man," Chikuni says of the grandfather. "Denis needs him, and he needs Denis."

Finally, Chikuni got the man to allow Denis to spend one day with him. "We were all nervous," remembers Maury, "but we knew this had to happen, so we prayed."

Denis did well on his one-day visit. That led to a weekend stay after which the grandfather said, "The boy has changed. He can stay here on holiday." Chikuni says that having Denis go home to face his family was tough, but "it was also a very freeing experience for him."

Chamunorwa, also 14, returned home in time to visit his father who was dying. He spent a week with the man, praying with him daily and thanking God for having given him such a fine father. The 14-year-old's prayer transformed his dying dad, and it blessed the boy as well. He looks forward to completing his education while at Lovemore House. Then he wants to go back to his home village to take care of the family that he left behind.

Centered in the gospel

The heart of Lovemore House is the gospel. Children are taught to pray by experiencing it daily in this tiny community of faith. Books of Bible stories are well-read favorites, and a video-tape of the Jesus Film in Shona language gets constant use.

Street life has severely damaged the Lovemore House children. Even after decompressing in a shelter where they experience having walls surround them, other children with whom they must interact, and minimal rules to obey, many have what Mendenhall calls "a wild streak" when they come to Lovemore. Having been severely abused, some bear deep psychological scars. Many have been caught up in a drug culture, working for pushers. Some have sniffed glue and petrol, and their capacity to think logically and sequentially has been severely damaged.

The odds are overwhelming. In Harare, alone, there are more than 3,000 children on the street, and to be saved, each one would require special care. "It's a real challenge," says Mendenhall, "but if we can save just one ... just one ..."

And so they have. One need only stand at the corner of Nelson Mandela and Angwa streets, where – like drought parched animals pawing at a dried up watering hole – children fight over bits and pieces of refuse from city rubbish piles. View that scene, enter the gates at Lovemore House, then remember the one who inspired this work: "Inasmuch as you have done it unto the least of these, you have done it unto me."

Some might say that what Chikuni and Mendenhall are doing is a mere drop in the bucket. In a sense, it is. But for the handful of children that enter their embrace, that drop is nothing less than the water of life.

Despite objections by many evangelicals and a Russian Orthodox delegation, the World Council of Churches approved a study of "diversity" of human sexuality, a course of action that many of the liberal leaders of the council hope will lead to an endorsement of homosexual relations.

Approval of the study came during a flurry of decisions, most with little or no debate, during the final day (Dec. 14, 1998) of the 50th anniversary assembly.

Lightning rod issue

Homosexuality was a lightning rod issue from the beginning of the council's assembly in Zimbabwe, a nation that has laws that make homosexual activity punishable by up to 10 years in prison. President Robert Mugabe suspended possible prosecution of people who attended the World Council of Churches but warned the WCC not to make homosexuality a major theme of the assembly.

The WCC did not spotlight homosexuality during its plenary sessions. However, a dozen padares featured the issue, and gay activists were front and center at press conferences.

Paul Sherry, president of the United Church of Christ in the United States, which ordains practicing homosexuals, brought the issue to the floor of the General Assembly on its closing day. Complaining that a resolution on human rights failed to mention discrimination against gays and lesbians, Sherry said, "Our support for human rights will ring increasingly hollow until we speak out against the violence done to our gay and lesbian brothers and sisters. Our silence in the midst of this violence is deafening." Sherry did not, however, seek to amend the resolution.

Later, when the program guidelines committee of the WCC identified the issue of human sexuality as one of seven areas for future WCC work, Russian Orthodox delegate Vladimir Shmaliy warned that "any move to develop a homosexual agenda would severely jeopardize Orthodox participation in the WCC." But his move to delete human sexuality from the report was soundly defeated.

y life without her would have been a poor thing." Lesslie Newbigin's tribute to Helen, his wife of 61 years, expresses precisely our sentiments on hearing of his passing from this life to the next. This profoundly Christian missionary, an ecumenist in the only sense that befits the Gospel, enriched us all.

For many years a missionary to the people of India, Newbigin knew what it was to be "multicultural" decades before postmodern pluralists impoverished that word.

He knew that the Gospel could not be captured by culture, but he also knew that the Gospel is expressed only within cultures

"Neither at the beginning, nor at any subsequent time, is there or can there be a Gospel that is not embodied in a culturally conditioned form of words," Newbigin said in his Warfield Lectures. He continued: "The idea that one can or could at any time separate out by some process of distillation a pure Gospel unadulterated by any cultural accretions is an illusion. It is, in fact, an abandonment of the Gospel, for the Gospel is about the word made flesh. ... Yet the Gospel, which is from the beginning to the end embodied in culturally conditioned forms, calls into question all cultures ..."

Newbigin helped us confess our inclination to export Western culture under the rubric of evangelism. Liberals with a disdain for anything that smacks of white, male eurocentrism cheered him mightily, until they realized that his words had also rendered untenable the Enlightenment premise on which their ideology depends.

Newbigin saw missions as a two-way street, for it is when we meet Jesus Christ as he appears in other cultures that we can best recognize the Jesus Christ who comes to us in our own. Cross-cultural, ecumenical encounters sharpen our discernment for recognizing the Word made flesh who dwells among us ... full of grace and truth.

Empowered by that conviction, Lesslie Newbigin led the International Missionary Council into the founding of the World Council of Churches. Rich with believers from every sector of the globe, this council, as Newbigin envisioned it, was to be a worldwide, self-critical witness to the Gospel. And in Amsterdam, on the day of its founding in 1948, it was.

But Newbigin's successors did not remain true to his vision. Displacing the Word made flesh with utopian passions for unity, World Council of Churches' leaders drew an ever-widening circle. Jesus of Nazareth became too particular, so a "Christ concept" came to the fore, expanding diversity's comfort zone by welcoming unfettered celebrations of the indigenous self.

In a 1996 London interview with *The Presbyterian Layman*, Newbigin discussed these things with a heavy heart. But even then he was not without hope. For he who recognized the inherent corruptibility of every human institution also trusted God-with-us, whose word offers life-giving possibilities to even the driest pile of bones.

While we have not yet seen that transformation in Newbigin's beloved World Council of Churches, we believe, as did he, that in God's good time, and in some form that is not yet apparent to us, we shall.

The Presbyterian Layman
March-April, 1998

On a street near the University of Zimbabwe, a billboard advertises instant connections to the World Wide Web. Beside it, a Zimbabwean woman roasts maize on the coals of a makeshift fire.

Zimbabweans are caught in a time warp between First- and Third-World realities. Having seen what modern technology can do, they want to be part of it. But few realize what that involves. One cannot be a First-World farmer, for example, while clinging to Third-World methodologies. An entire way of thinking must shift.

Culture clash

The World Council of Churches faces similar dichotomies, for members of the organization are juggling incompatible visions of its nature and purpose. Some identify with the council's founding vision: a worldwide association of Christians who are passionate to proclaim Jesus Christ in every land. Others see the council as a socio-political entity, a non-governmental organization whose powers transcend any single nation-state and impact the policies of them all.

For three decades, the latter vision has been in vogue. "Our people need a conversion experience," said William Phipps, moderator of the United Church of Canada, at the WCC Assembly. "Conversion has to do with economic relationships," he said. "Economic relationships are central to our understanding of the faith."

'Global governance'

The anthropology promoted by current WCC leaders calls human beings (especially if they are "indigenous") intrinsically good. It is only the imposition of socioeconomic structures that turns their lives toward evil. Thus the mission of the church is politics. Jesus is the great liberator who inspires his followers to topple governments deemed unjust and control corporations by means of "global governance."

This vision of WCC leaders led them to bankroll guerrilla warfare in Africa, support Castro's regime in Cuba, the Sandinistas in Nicaragua, rebel forces in El Salvador, and Soviet-inspired destabilization throughout the Third World. Peace can only come, declared the WCC, where a managed economy is imposed.

To the WCC's embarrassment, every socialist scheme that it supported has failed. No government lauded by the WCC has been able to feed its own people. The Sandinistas were thrown out in internationally-monitored, free elections. The Soviet Union crumbled. Yet with unabashed zeal, it continues to call for more of the same. Third

World debt issues, income redistribution, and the imposition of "global governance" on transnational corporations took center stage in the WCC's Harare meeting.

A different vision

But in Harare there were also signs of hope. Moderator Aram I admitted in his opening address that the WCC can claim to be only "an" ecumenical movement, and that unless it addresses the causes of its decline, a greater ecumenism will pass it by.

Another sign of hope is a growing emphasis on missions, particularly among the rapidly growing African and Asian communions. In the Assembly's plenary session, Presbyterian leader Marian McClure expressed thanks to the delegates for having included a strong missions statement in the WCC's priorities for the next seven years.

Some WCC leaders, following former Presbyterian staff member Mary Ann Lundy's lead, had wanted the WCC to include non-Christian groups with compatible socioeconomic goals. That move was rejected when the assembly stated that it will limit its partnerships to those who affirm Trinitarian faith.

The Presbyterian influence

Presbyterians bear grave responsibility for the WCC's misguided policies, for that is the direction that many of our representatives have advocated. Perusing Presbyterian delegations over the past three decades, one discovers many of our most liberal personalities, the very persons who have led our own denomination into severe decline.

Many Presbyterians who appeared in Harare in December, 1988, represented a who's who of ReImagining God personalities, Voices of Sophia supporters, Social Witness Policy advocates, and radical feminists. In no sense could one say that this group as a whole represented the rank and file membership of our denomination, yet theirs was the image that we projected to the world church.

Where do we go from here?

If we didn't have a World Council of Churches, we would surely have to create one. Christians throughout the world need some organization that facilitates our getting together and sharing the gospel as it is proclaimed and lived in our cultures. The mechanisms of a World Council of Churches are also important when churches respond to the needs of fellow Christians in areas where war or disaster strikes. As the stated clerk noted in his column in *The Presbyterian Layman's* January-

February, 1999, edition, the WCC gives Presbyterians an opportunity to work, as Jesus commanded, for a biblically-based unity in Christ. The problem of the WCC is not that it exists, but that its controlling vision for the past thirty years – a vision heavily influenced by Presbyterian representatives – has been fatally flawed. Thus, while we believe that our denomination's financial contribution to the WCC should be reduced to a level comparable to that given by other USA denominations, we do not advocate abandoning the WCC. Instead, we call on the Presbyterian evangelical community – members who care about proclaiming the gospel to the ends of the earth – to take a renewed interest in this ecumenical organization, to stand for election as Presbyterian Church (USA) representatives, and to reclaim the great missionary vision that gave the WCC its birth.

Tuesday, December 1, 1998 10:40 PM

Dear PLC staff:

Just a note to tell you that we have arrived safely in Harare.

The trip was generally uneventful. Flight to London was smooth and being able to sleep a few hours in Gatwick's Travel Inn was a luxury.

No phones in our room at Travel Inn so email was not a possibility. I tried to hook up my HP portable printer to print out a version of my first article that could be faxed from the desk, but the outlet blew up with a shower of sparks and our end of the hotel went dark (just a wee bit embarrassing!) Apparently the conflagration didn't do anything to the HP printer but it may have been the end of Patty's voltage converter. That means we probably won't be blow drying any hair over here.

Fortunately, I ran into "Mona" who took pity on me, accepted a copy of my draft article from a floppy disk, and ran it thorough her computer. That got me a printout to send to you.

The all-night flight to Harare was interesting. I was sandwiched between Patty (who dozed most of the way) and Christine, an attorney from Paris who is a member of the Reformed Church and thinks John Calvin was a hoot. We struggled with her broken English and my ridiculous French. She told me that what drew her to the World Council of Churches was its devotion to "causes." She was very pleased regarding the WCC's role in South African black liberation, though she's not too high on Mugabe right now. He was her hero, but lately some of the shine has come off of his halo. Try as I might, I couldn't get her to see that a direct application of revolutionary ideology to politics leads to despotism. She's a thoroughgoing socialist, and she won't have it any other way.

The plane (a 747) was full of WCC folks, tons of regional council of churches types wearing slogan-covered T shirts. For many people on this plane, this was like old home week, lots of hugging and backslapping.

Met a beautiful young black woman from Rwanda, wife of a Presbyterian minister. She escaped to London on the eve of the war and spent several months not knowing if her husband was alive. He survived, but all other members of her family were killed. Both she and her husband now live in London. She's a journalist and a lovely person with a well-tested faith. I look forward to knowing her better.

The Harare airport is a mess. Looks like a World-War II corrugated tin hangar. Hot as Hades. Very officious, military-looking immigration agents who seemed to enjoy making foreigners jump through hoops. When we arrived we were told that on this very morning (what a coincidence!) the President (that's the way they refer to Mugabe) had declared a new law that we were now required to pay an entrance fee of $60, and only US dollars were acceptable. I had brought $100 in cash, two $20 bills that we knew would be required for our exit from the country (the government will not accept its own money), and exactly $60 in one-dollar bills. So I started counting out $60, and the official made me go to the end of the line because I was inconveniencing him with my form of payment. When I finally got back to the booth, he re-counted the sixty, pausing to straighten out each bent corner

and turn each bill in the same direction. Then
another uniformed official came into the booth
and they discussed the difficulties they
experienced with inconsiderate foreigners who
paid in such small bills. Then the second
official proceeded to count out the sixty again,
just checking up on his colleague. The
temperature in the hangar was somewhere near 90
and my own internal thermostat blew its top, but
I smiled and we all got through it.

I made a contact with Harare's control data and
(if all goes well) we will get my internet access
account set up on Wednesday morning. In the
meantime, I can fax to you through the hotel's
business center, but at $5.00 a page, that's a
little pricey.

Patty and I slept much of the afternoon, trying
to recover from our second all-night flight and a
7-hour time zone change. Then we went out on the
street to get our bearings and do a little
currency trading. The Zimbabwean/US exchange rate
was 28/1 when we left the USA. Today it was 35/1.
How 'bout that for inflation?

We made it back to the hotel just ahead of our
first African rainstorm. Never have I seen such
an event. The sky was ablaze with celestial
fireworks and huge drops of rain appeared in
sheets, propelled by a wind that hurled it
horizontally. The streets filled up and were
somewhere between ankle and knee deep in torrents
that couldn't drain away fast enough. It was wild
and quick - all over in maybe thirty minutes.
For dinner tonight I ate crocodile croquettes
(with a hot sauce) as an appetizer and ostrich
for my main course. The crocodile was somewhat
tasteless (I guess that's why they brought out
the sauce) but the ostrich, a very dark meat, had
a real kick to it. Patty stuck with grilled
vegetables. The whole tab was $350.00 Zimbabwean

dollars (about $10 in our money). I thought I
ought to let my tummy settle down a bit from the
trip before I tackle the wart hog. Maybe
tomorrow.

That's about it for now.

Parker

By Stephen Brown
Ecumenical News International

GENEVA, January 27, 1999 – The World Council of Churches has added its voice to international concern about claims that two Zimbabwean journalists were tortured by Zimbabwean military police and secret service agents because of a newspaper article about an alleged plot against the Harare government.

Yesterday 26 January, riot police in Zimbabwe's capital, Harare, used tear gas to break up a demonstration protesting against the alleged torture of the two journalists. About 200 police officers armed with rifles, shotguns and tear gas surrounded the parliament building and closed off the city's Africa Unity Square.

The two journalists – Mark Chavunduka, editor of the Standard, an independent newspaper, and Ray Choto, a senior reporter – were freed on bail last week after being charged with publishing false information capable of causing alarm and despondency. After being released, they said that they had been subjected to torture – including electric shocks to their genitals - by military police and agents of Zimbabwe's Central Intelligence Organisation.

Reporters in Harare said that the two journalists were limping when they were released, and that their hands and feet were severely swollen.

A WCC spokesperson, John Newbury, told ENI that the forms of torture that the two journalists had alleged – holding victims' heads under water and applying electric shock during interrogation – "were identified by the WCC nearly 25 years ago as clear early warning signs of impending widespread and systematic human rights abuse in militarised societies."

The two journalists said that they had been tortured to make them reveal their sources for a report this month in the Standard that 23 army officers had been arrested in December for plotting a coup against the government of President Robert Mugabe.

The newspaper stated that the officers were plotting a coup because of Zimbabwe's involvement in the civil war in the Democratic Republic of Congo. Many Zimbabweans believe that their country, which is facing severe financial difficulties, cannot afford to take part in the war. Some media reports claim Zimbabwe's involvement costs $US1 million a day. Last month, the WCC held its seven-yearly assembly in Harare, an event which brought up to 5000 people from around the world to Zimbabwe. During the assembly, which was addressed by President Mugabe, WCC officials repeatedly declined to comment on allegations of violations of human and civil rights in Zimbabwe, saying that it was a long-standing WCC practice not to criticise governments of countries hosting WCC meetings. The reports of torture have prompted the Commonwealth Human Rights Initiative, an international non-governmental charity which works to promote human rights in Commonwealth countries, to call for an independent investigation into the allegations. The British government has also called on the Zimbabwean government to investigate the claims, and, if warranted, to press charges against those responsible.

PLC Publications
Raising the standard

Standing Firm: Reclaiming Christian Faith in Times of Controversy, by Parker T. Williamson. $12 for single copies. $6 in quantities of 10 or more. Plus shipping and handling.

> A riveting account of how the Nicene Creed emerged out of fourth-century controversies. Thomas F. Torrance, professor emeritus of theology at Edinburgh, Scotland: "One of the most brilliant, refreshing and helpful books concerned with the heart and centre of the life and witness of the church that has happened in recent years."

I Believe ... The Apostles' Creed for The Third Millennium, by Robert P. Mills. $5 for single copies. $4.50 in quantities of 10 or more. Plus shipping and handling.

> A powerful commentary on the Apostles' Creed. This study helps the reader know more fully and personally the Trinitarian God – Father, Son and Holy Spirit. Designed for use by Sunday school classes and other study groups.

Whom Alone We Worship and Serve: What the Bible Teaches about God, by Robert P. Mills. $4.50 for single copies. $4.00 in quantities of 10 or more. Plus shipping and handling.

> This study interweaves the witness of Scripture, the insights of scholars from early church fathers to current evangelical commentators, and the historic Reformed perspective. Now being used by Sunday school classes, Presbyterian Women and Bible study groups.

To order copies: Call toll-free **1-800-368-0110**
PLC Publications / P.O. Box 2210 / Lenoir, NC 28645-2210

For more information about publications and complete news about the PCUSA, visit the official Internet site of the Presbyterian Lay Committee at www.layman.org